The

5

Essentials of
ORGANIZATIONAL
EXCELLENCE

Maximizing Schoolwide Student
Achievement and Performance

Lawrence L. Marazza

CORWIN PRESS, INC.
A Sage Publications Company
Thousand Oaks, California

For information:

Corwin Press, Inc.
A Sage Publications Company
2455 Teller Road
Thousand Oaks, California 91320
www.corwinpress.com

Sage Publications Ltd.
6 Bonhill Street
London EC2A 4PU
United Kingdom

Sage Publications India Pvt. Ltd.
B-42, Panchsheel Enclave
Post Box 4109
New Delhi 110 017 India

Printed in the United States of America

Library of Congress Cataloging-in-Publication Data

Marazza, Lawrence L.
The five essentials of organizational excellence : maximizing schoolwide student achievement and performance / by Lawrence L. Marazza.
    p. cm.
Includes bibliographical references and index.
ISBN 0-7619-3954-7 (Cloth : acid-free paper) — ISBN 0-7619-3955-5
(Paper : acid-free paper)
   1. School management and organization—United States. 2. School improvement programs—United States. 3. Academic achievement-United States. I. Title.
LB2806.M225 2003
371.2—dc21

                                    2003009310

This book is printed on acid-free paper.

03   04   05   06   07   7   6   5   4   3   2   1

Acquisitions Editor:	Robert D. Clouse
Editorial Assistant:	Jingle Vea
Production Editor:	Julia Parnell
Copy Editor:	Teresa Herlinger
Proofreader:	Colleen Brennan
Typesetter:	C&M Digitals (P) Ltd.
Indexer:	Rachel Rice
Cover Designer:	Tracy E. Miller
Production Artist:	Lisa Miller

Contents

Preface

The Five Essentials to Organizational Excellence is the result of my experiences over twenty-six years as a public school superintendent. My journey as a superintendent can best be summed up as a continuous search for "a better way." Accountability for improved student achievement has long been a national goal and served as the main criterion for the decisions I made and the recommendations I offered to school boards on a daily basis. I was on a constant search for a system, a program, an initiative, and a solution to the problems and challenges we faced regarding student achievement. As I look back, I realize that, like most people, I learned more from my failures than from my successes. It could be that what I learned from my failures *led* to my successes. In any event, what I now know is that organizational development in public schools is an emerging and continuous process. Furthermore, organizational development represents the cornerstone of increased learning potential for students in American classrooms today.

I learned quickly that my effectiveness as a school leader was greatly enhanced by collaboration with those around me. What began as improvement of my own collaborative skills grew to become the main focus of human resource development in the school districts I served. What began as confrontation and "we-they" attitudes between my administration and parents grew into a positive and productive engagement of parents and other community members.

More times than not, my search for "a better way" took me to unconventional sources. Applying private-sector practices to public schools was very successful for me, although it is not a widespread practice even today. Once I started down this road, I discovered and invented programs and systems to improve learning potential that would never have been experienced without the journey. Innovation in public schools is not encouraged by those still operating under traditional organizational management practices. As Margaret Wheatley so aptly points out in her book *Leadership and the New Science*, "I believe that we have only just begun the process of discovering and inventing the new organizational forms that will inhabit the twenty-first century. To be responsible inventors and discoverers, though, we need the courage to let go of the old world" (1994, p. 5). What category of organizations could and should better benefit from inventing new forms of organization than public schools whose business is teaching and learning?

We are driven to discover and invent new organizational forms primarily because of the dramatic changes in our society—changes reflected in our public schools. Our organizational forms must be transformed in order to

1. Effectively meet the challenges of ever-increasing diversity in the student population as well as the workforce.

2. Capitalize on growing diversity in the population and the workforce as an ever-expanding source of capability and strength for the organization.

The responsibility for leadership has become too demanding for one person to shoulder. While there has been much written and debated about the leadership needed in organizations today, without question leadership is currently being redefined to tap into the new leadership potential of all the stakeholders of schools across our nation. In American public education, the redefinition of this leadership is most critical in the position of the school principal. School principals are in the position to most effectively facilitate much-needed collaborative leadership to the benefit of students across this nation.

When I began to commit to writing my thoughts regarding what was required to transform our public schools into learning organizations that so many people have dreamed about and have shared with me over the years, it occurred to me that, first and foremost, we had to ready ourselves for profound change. To do so requires an unprecedented change in how we think about organizing for learning and decision making regarding schools. As we think differently about school organizations, we must address the issue of leaving behind those organizational forms that either worked for a less complex time, or never worked but were sustained over time because of a pervasive "mindlessness" regarding meeting the changing needs of our stakeholders.

I have attempted to bring meaning to the integration of what I have determined are the Five Essentials of school transformation. Planning Strategically, Benchmarking for Excellence, Leading Collaboratively, Engaging the Public, and Governing by Standards constitute the building blocks of a new form of organizing for public schools. Each system or process, when implemented independently of the others, contributes to increased effectiveness of the organization in terms of student achievement. Because of the overlapping nature of the Five Essentials, when implemented as a whole, their contribution to organizational effectiveness is significantly greater.

There is no question that it takes courage to cast off old ways that do not work and take that leap of faith required to invent and adopt new organizational forms. This book was written to make that leap as short and comfortable as possible for those courageous enough to let go of the old ways.

Acknowledgments

This book is the result of many factors interwoven across decades of public service that have left me wiser and humbler. Major themes of my life experience surfaced as I began the development of the composition of this book. These themes formed the essence of the message most important to me and most important to the accomplishment of organizational excellence. Consequently, the Five Essentials represents a translation of these themes into both a philosophy and a practical guide to achieving school organizational excellence. Upon further reflection, I realized that there was no theme more important to the achievement of organizational excellence than the subject of the relationships among and between people—members of the organization.

The Five Essentials surfaced as the conduit through which to maximize the effectiveness and the quality of these relationships. Although this understanding, this focus on relationships, has a natural, underlying simplicity, to recognize it—moreover, to know it—requires the assistance of others. It is with a deep sense of gratitude that I recognize others who helped point the way for me and, by so doing, underscored further the importance of relationships between people.

A special note of thanks goes to Dr. Burton Gorman who was my mentor and who inspired me from the beginning of my journey. His encouragement led me down a wonderful road that would not have otherwise been taken.

At the Weatherhead School of Management at Case Western Reserve University, my colleagues in the Professional Fellows program contributed a meaningful sense of inquiry and a mix of perspectives that included an excitement about exploring possibilities. In particular, special gratitude is expressed to Susan Case, professor of organizational behavior, who taught me how to know myself and by so doing became my friend. Also, I thank David Kolb of the Weatherhead School for introducing me to the power of conversation. Stu Klein at the Center for the Advancement of Cooperation Between Labor and Management (currently the Labor-Management Relations Center) at Cleveland State University provided meaningful insights into conflict management and problem-solving skills development.

Ted Sanders, president of the Education Commission of the States, offered proven insights about educational leadership and taught me the meaning of the courage to lead. Faye Cake exemplified personal courage and professional commitment and taught me the importance of relationships.

Gratitude is also expressed to Robert Clouse, Senior Acquisitions Editor at Corwin Press, who believed enough in my work to pilot its course. And to all the editors at Corwin with whom I am now forming quality relationships, I want to express my appreciation.

Countless educators and school board members believed in me and supported me through the years. I would like to thank David Schilling, Jim Rhodebeck, George Heath, Barbara Stone, Steve Franko, Paul Pendelton, David Chandler, Pat Hardwick, Connie Hauser, Don McClarren, Boyd Epperson, Ed Epperson, Paul Sabatino, Paul Friedman, Eugene Griffith, Martin Essex, Franklin Walter, Don Lewis, Gary Frankhouse, Jim Moffitt, William Burcham, Stan Lasky, John Ely, Jr., Lois Herrmann, Dennis Chrustic, Susan Foley, John Richards, Tom Wittmer, and Thea Jasper. To all the parents, teachers, and administrators who formed productive collaborations with me and each other, to the benefit of children in the schools I served, I am especially grateful.

Without the encouragement of my family, this work would not have been accomplished. A special thank you is offered to Mark and Karen Marazza.

Corwin Press gratefully acknowledges the contributions of the following reviewers:

Dr. Robert Blake
Principal
Mainland Regional High School
Linwood, NJ

Ann Charles
Principal
Portsmouth High School
Portsmouth, OH

Frank Rudnesky
Principal
Belhaven Middle School
Linwood, NJ

About the Author

Lawrence Marazza is the president and founder of the Lighthouse Management Group, a training and management consulting firm located in Russell, Ohio, and focusing on the development of high-performing school districts and quality assurance programs for public sector organizations. His career in education spans more than thirty years, including twenty-six years as a superintendent of schools for three school districts located in two different states. He has also served as an elementary and secondary teacher, college instructor, and public administrator.

Throughout his career, he has been able to apply private-sector leadership initiatives and practices to public schools. During his tenure as a superintendent, he established partnerships with businesses and institutions of higher learning. Through these partnerships, he developed leadership training programs for parents, teachers, school administrators and other stakeholders in public education. Under his leadership, school district alliances with businesses and universities have produced innovative programs and practices that have resulted in significantly improved learning opportunities for students, as well as the formation of collaborative teams of public-school stakeholders meaningfully involved in school decision making.

Dr. Marazza was named a "Distinguished Graduate in Teacher Education" by Mount Union College. He is also a Professional Fellow with the Weatherhead School of Management at Case Western Reserve University. He has served as the administrative representative on evaluation teams across the country for the National Council for the Accreditation of Teacher Education. He also serves as a Senior Associate with Proact Search, Inc. In addition, he is a contributing author to *The Power of Public Engagement: A Beacon of Hope for America's Schools* (1999).

This book is dedicated in loving memory to the two people most influential in my life—my mother and father, Bernice and James Marazza. My father taught me the value of discipline and my mother taught me the value of love.

Introduction

Collaborative Leadership Team Development

The Nature of a Lack of Leadership and the Need for the Five Essentials

For years now, American public schools have been criticized and judged unsuccessful. Many commissions and a constant stream of studies have concluded that major reform and reorganization of our schools is long overdue. Indeed, billions of dollars and isolated and independent initiatives have been devoted to demonstrating improvement. But nowhere have we demonstrated improvement on a broad and sweeping front. The need to improve student achievement is at the core of this movement.

No other profession demands so little additional training and professional development, once a member of the profession is certified or licensed, than public school teaching. Teacher salary schedules reward each additional year of experience with step increases, but experience alone is not nearly enough to guarantee improved teaching. When we examine the dollars budgeted for human resource development in public education in light of other professions, public education pales by comparison.

Research, as well as common sense, indicates that the building principal is the key to successful school transformation. The principal's educational leadership style is crucial to developing high-performance schools. How he or she relates to parents and teachers, how he or she makes educational decisions, and what skills of leadership he or she brings to the position of building principal are major factors in the transformation of schools.

We have learned much about the profiles of high-performing organizations over the past ten years. There is no reason why we can't apply what we have learned to public schools. What Peter Senge, in *The Fifth Discipline,* describes as "learning organizations" surely applies to schools. He describes a "learning organization" as, "an organization that is continually expanding its capacity to create its future" (1990, p. 14). What organization can better build a learning community than a public school whose business is learning? Although many schools and school districts have implemented legitimate programs designed to bring about reformation of the schools with learning as the centerpiece, they all too often have failed to link or connect the building blocks of organizational development. What are these essentials to the transformation of schools and how do we recognize them?

If we consider the most controversial issues surrounding public schools and public school reform, the most frequent criticisms revolve around fundamental flaws in the organizational structure of public schools. Ineffective governance, unresponsiveness to customer needs, the absence of meaningful standards of excellence reflected in daily work, and a lack of meaningful public involvement form the core of basic criticisms of public schools in America today.

Validation of this observation can be found in the popularity of the charter school movement across America. The political climate in which state legislators formulate charter school legislation and the manner in which local charter schools form and operate are both designed to address these basic criticisms of public schools. Their success is yet to be determined, and the danger here is that we may be "throwing out the baby with the bath water." When Henry Steele Comminger, noted historian, once said, "Our schools have kept us free," his reference was to our *public* schools, with their noble tradition in American history.

The causes of many of these criticisms are embedded in the way schools are operated and governed. Mindless adherence to organizational rules and regulations that reflect narrowly drawn guidelines is the result of the autonomous thinking of hierarchal organizations.

Collaborative organizations produce a much wider range of possibilities, coupled with the combined wisdom of all the stakeholders, rather than the single-mindedness that reflects the nature of traditional public school organizations. As a result of these kinds of organizational shortcomings, representatives of public schools appear at times to be insensitive and unresponsive. Many times I have observed members of school boards at a public meeting trying to defend the indefensible, always to their own embarrassment, but not knowing any other way. People don't know what they don't know.

Why is it that invariably in schools, especially elementary schools, parents argue with building principals about the assignment of their child to a specific teacher at the beginning of every school year? Without a school district program of benchmarking "best teaching practices" accruing to the benefit of the improvement of all teachers, parents institute their own informal program of "best teachers" through "word of mouth" with other parents. Building principals in such situations are making decisions by the authority of their position, not through any process that offers the opportunity to engage parents in legitimate and shared decision making. The issues surrounding school reform often revolve around school governance. At the governance level, we often hear the terms *standards* and *planning*. Planning involving *whom* and standards written by *what process* become the crucial questions.

Public schools have suffered from a top-down bureaucracy that evaluates with little or no involvement from the educators evaluated, that makes decisions affecting the public with little or no meaningful public participation, and that substitutes planning a budget for budgeting a plan. Leadership is not developed for education. It falls to school boards to choose leaders.

But *how* do school boards choose leadership? What are their criteria? Should we recognize standardized criteria for selection? Would doing so erode local control? How do school boards develop effective leadership? This book is offered as a practical approach to developing leadership at both the school and school district level. The "Five Essentials" for school transformation are described, highlighted for their importance, and profiled in a practical and integrated manner.

TRANSFORMATIONAL LEADERSHIP

This book attempts to merge a vision and achievement of organizational excellence with the engagement of the stakeholders on a personal level. If we are to achieve excellence in America's schools, we must develop the skills required on an individual stakeholder basis. But it is school leaders who must facilitate and create the environment for the development of these skills.

Indeed, transformational leadership requires this: Leadership in this context must become relational. Unlike requirements of the past, leaders today must communicate visions of the organization understandable to all stakeholders. In this sense, it is the responsibility of the school principal to continuously engage in conversations with teachers and parents, the underlying thread of which is to keep the guiding vision of the school constantly present and clearly embraced in the daily decision making of teachers and parents as they work toward the achievement of that vision.

In addition, the nature of leadership in traditional gatherings of the stakeholders in schools such as open houses, PTA meetings, and school planning committees must change. The school principal's role in this newly defined context is not to bring rigid rules or inflexible structures to these gatherings. Rather, the principal must constantly shape the organization by clearly communicating the purpose of the school. Furthermore, the principal who is communicating in this relational manner must then allow for what may seem to be a disorderly and independent path that individual stakeholders (parents and teachers) travel to eventually make their unique contribution to the attainment of that vision. Principals today must develop a strong tolerance for ambiguity as those he or she works with make a combined wisdom contribution to the accomplishment of the school mission. As the principal's tolerance for ambiguity grows, trust in the stakeholders deepens.

As the school principal develops a leadership profile that emphasizes relationships and clarity of purpose of the school, he or she must also set the stage for the development of skills within the stakeholders essential to the achievement of the school vision. A newly defined leadership profile and the development of essential skills within the stakeholders go hand in hand on the road to achieving high performance in America's schools.

Within these pages, I have focused on both the processes and products required to achieve excellence in America's schools. What are the essential skills? How do we sustain both the development and achievement of these skills?

NEW SKILLS REQUIRED

Educators today live and work in a public school organizational structure and design that is based on needs from a sociology of the past. The sociology of today has changed dramatically. We need to design school organizations capable of meeting the needs reflected by a current sociology, including a reformulated definition of stakeholder needs.

First, let's face the lack of success of schools today. Second, let's learn the skills and understand the organizational concepts underlying high performance in public schools. Most important, let's understand and accept that meaningful change and meaningful organizational improvement are the result of educational stakeholders engaging with other stakeholders on a personal and therefore meaningful basis. Finding personal meaning in the process of achieving organizational excellence is fundamental to developing high-performing schools. Margaret Wheatley says it best in her book *Leadership and the New Science:*

> First, I no longer believe that organizations can be changed by imposing a model developed elsewhere. . . . Second . . . the new physics cogently explains that there is no objective reality out there waiting to reveal its secrets. . . . There is only what we create through our engagement with others. (1992, p. 7)

Organizations live, grow, and develop. They are a macrocosm of their constituent parts—their stakeholders. This concept is a long stretch from the historical view of organizations that is best described as mechanistic, with little or no recognition of the human potential and creative enterprise produced by meaningful engagement of its stakeholders qualified in the essential skills of the transformation of organizations. The creative possibilities of developing critical skills within all public school stakeholders, heretofore reserved for specific school district departments or private sector enterprise, are limitless.

WHAT IF?

What would be the result for organizations if we were able to develop transformational skills within their stakeholders? What if industry best practices (benchmarking) were filtered through the unique characteristics of each school? What if all the stakeholders brought the skills of strategic planning to their responsibilities within the organization? What if all stakeholders benefited from interaction with other stakeholders through their own collaborative leadership skills as well as the skills of those in charge of the organization? What if the principles and skills of public engagement were made a fundamental tenet of the everyday practice of working with or relating to other stakeholders? What if jointly conceived and mutually developed standards of excellence served as the criteria for everyday decision making, relied upon not only by those at the governance level, but also by every other stakeholder, especially building principals at the school sites.

WHAT IF, INDEED?

Then students and student achievement would thrive. There would be no limit to personal and organizational achievement. Most important, the self-renewing nature of the conceptual understanding and everyday practice of these skills would ensure the future success of the organization as well. The Five Essentials have a synchronous relationship, one to the other. Graduate schools of educational administration do not offer in their curriculum the chance to develop the skills necessary to build the organizational capacity to improve student achievement opportunities at the local school level. Within these pages, I have outlined the Five Essentials to bringing about improved student achievement. I offer this as an ongoing process that invites personal commitment and investment on the part of all the stakeholders of a school or school district. Planning, benchmarking, leading, engaging, and governing are described and developed as collaborative processes but, more important, they are presented in an integrated fashion.

As I developed the Five Essentials, I left behind some of the antiquated mythology regarding sacred cows in public schools. It is an outdated notion that there is nothing to gain by combining the talents of elementary teachers with those of teachers from secondary schools. Cross-functional teams of elementary and secondary teachers can produce combined wisdom for the benefit of student learning unattainable otherwise. Partnership between public schools and universities should *not* be limited to the traditional forms of student teaching and administrative internships. The teacher's union can be very helpful by being involved in the process of building school budgets and helping plan for the future of the school district. We must recognize that empowering others is the best path to self-empowerment. Educators operate with a natural affinity for one another provided a climate of mutual trust has been established. Some of the skills I learned in problem-solving negotiations in public schools were indeed a forerunner to the concepts presented here and the skills I've identified as necessary to the transformation of schools. Margaret Wheatley describes the new dance we must learn:

> I would be excited to encounter people delighted by surprises instead of the ones I now meet who are scared to death of them. . . . Surprise *is* the only route to discovery, the only path we can take if we're to search out the important principles that can govern our work. This dance of this universe extends to all the relationships we have. Knowing the steps ahead of time is not important; being willing to engage with the music and move freely onto the dance floor is what's the key. (1992, p. 142)

Teams of people working collaboratively create new knowledge. In order to assemble the necessary new knowledge to transform public schools into learning organizations, we must learn the skills developed by the implementation of the Five Essentials. Replacing administrative practice from the past with the flexibility of new organizational forms allows us to capitalize upon the unpredictable in productive ways. Then, and only then, will we be able to welcome the surprises the unpredictable will bring us.

SUMMARY

Each of the Five Essentials for the transformation of schools offers a path to organizational high performance. However, achieving organizational excellence begins with the quality of the relationships among and between the organizational stakeholders. Although there are significant differences between school organizations and private-sector business, there is much for schools to learn by studying characteristics of high-performing, non-public organizations.

One needs to look no further than the swelling charter school movement across our nation to understand some of the dissatisfaction experienced by public school students and their parents today. The "top-down" bureaucratic form of organization with little or no stakeholder involvement still characterizes many of our public school districts. Consequently, transforming schools begins with "unlearning" old ways.

New knowledge generated by teams of people working collaboratively forms the basis of the replacement of administrative practices from the past with the flexibility of new organizational forms necessary to achieve excellence in a world best characterized by an ever-increasing diversity of organizational stakeholders.

If we are to achieve excellence in our schools, then we must address the issue of what skills our stakeholders are lacking and what skills must become the cornerstone of our staff development efforts. Because no school representative interfaces more with all public school stakeholders on a daily basis than school building principals, their position is a major focus of this book. Developing these skills within building principals is the key to initiating the transformation of schools. These skills and the benefits they bring to any organization are presented for those willing to part with traditional forms and practices in an effort to transform their organization by tapping the human potential of their stakeholders. The missing essential skills are introduced in Chapter 1.

1

The Missing Essential Connections to Educational Excellence

The past has never been a good guide to those futures, but without conceptual skills we seldom had any choice but to go on doing what we did. Now we can, and must, take better charge of our own destinies—and learn the skills that allow us to do it.

—Charles Handy (1996)

UNCONNECTED SYSTEMS

Today there exists a disconnect in public education between governance, strategic planning, public engagement, standards of excellence, leadership, and daily operations. It appears to occur without any thought given to these ultimately important ties essential to the accomplishment of the school or school district mission. Maximizing and realizing the potential for student achievement demands that educators understand and implement, both operationally and strategically, the Five Essentials for transforming a school, some of which are taken from private sector management practices. Nowhere is it more important that these essential skills be evident than at the school building level. Moreover, at the building level, nowhere is it more important that these skills be evident than in the position of school principal. What may seem to be a rather random and at times chaotic interaction or lack of interaction among and between the Five Essentials can be harnessed to work in concert so as to create a stronger sense of meaning, commitment, and common purpose for the stakeholders of a school or school district. We have seen, over the past decade, school district after school district and the schools within those school districts engage in the process and discipline of strategic planning or public engagement only to become frustrated because of the disconnection between the school board and various groups, such as teachers or parents, when the process is "complete." The point is that both the development and implementation of these processes is never complete. Rather, they become a system with which to govern and manage a school or school district.

The Five Essentials incorporate the following components to achieving educational excellence as well as the delineation of the connections among and between them:

- Plan strategically
- Benchmark for excellence
- Lead collaboratively
- Engage the public
- Govern by standards

The Five Essentials examine how school goals can best be established and who should establish them. They analyze the relationships among and between the stakeholders of public education and what defines excellence within these relationships. The establishment of benchmarks of excellence for both basic and advanced educational programs is also analyzed. Using excellence as the standard, the Five Essentials incorporate conclusions regarding who are the customers and how we can best serve them. It is also important to consider how we can best approach local determinants within individual schools or school districts. Most important, the Five Essentials focus upon how all the components of excellence integrate to maximize learning opportunities for students.

THINKING AND PLANNING STRATEGICALLY

The impact of semantics in conversation among the stakeholders of a school or school district is a major factor, which threads its way through all of the essentials of excellence. People talk about what they think about and they act on what they talk about. Without thought, there can be no conversation. Without conversation, there should be no action. The quality of these thoughts and conversations determines the quality of decisions put into action.

At the school building level, cross-functional teams of teachers, administrators, and parents can use their combined wisdom to quickly flush out a solution to many problems that are never solved otherwise. Building principals must be possessed with the skills to facilitate this process, for it most appropriately falls to them to accept this responsibility.

Thinking and planning strategically begins with conversation. These conversations must be rich with the initiation and development of ideas. "Conjoining conversation" techniques are helpful to engage the best thinking for any problem facing the organization. These techniques serve as a precursor to collaboration and the development of collaborative leadership skills. Indeed, the beginnings of the development of collaboration skills are at the heart of conjoining conversation. While the application of conjoining conversation skills represents a good beginning of the process of productively combining the wisdom of organizational stakeholders, it is the contribution of conjoining conversation to the development of collaborative leadership skills that, in turn, helps produce an ongoing collaborative process that is most notable. Collaborative leadership skills contribute to the process most capable of producing the combined wisdom of the participants on a continuous basis.

Defining directions for engaging in productive conversation is important in order for the group to stay on task. The objective is to develop the environment in which a proactive conversation incorporating the combined wisdom of the group can be accomplished. The following list suggests the first steps of conjoining conversation. In almost every instance, one of the following will be most appropriate for the task at hand:

1. Define the problem that needs to be solved, then solve it.

2. Describe the challenge that needs to be met, then meet it.

3. Share the ideas that need to be developed, then develop them.

Once the problem is defined, the challenge described, or the ideas shared, the following suggested directions for establishing conjoining conversation should be applied:

1. Name a member of the group to be the group facilitator. The facilitator should be the group member most respected for his or her objectivity and fair mindedness.

2. Open discussion regarding possible solutions to problems, ways to meet challenges, or the development of ideas previously discussed into workable organizational improvements. The facilitator should encourage the sharing of "partial ideas." It is not necessary to have a well thought out idea before a participant shares it. One idea from one person often triggers another idea from another. This represents the beginning of producing combined wisdom.

3. Constructively criticize ideas but be careful not to criticize the originator. The purpose of conjoining conversation is to explore all possibilities, and the participants need to feel free to make suggestions without fear of potentially embarrassing criticism from others. Participants need to feel comfortable to share their thoughts without concern that these thoughts may not be among the best offered. The "building power" of one idea on top of another is crucial to the development of combined wisdom. A "bad idea" in isolation may become very helpful in tandem with another idea.

4. Once everyone has had the opportunity to contribute all their ideas on the problem or challenge, it is the responsibility of the facilitator to begin linking ideas together, based on similarity or potential for solving the problem or meeting the challenge.

5. When the conjoined conversation is complete, the facilitator should open discussion regarding which ideas offer the most promise. Deciding by consensus, a list of the most promising ideas is then compiled.

6. Next, the facilitator should initiate the development of action plans by guiding the group through a repeat of steps 2 through 5 above, focusing upon the development of the most promising ideas into action plans.

Conjoining conversation levels positional power. Everyone must be viewed as on "equal footing." The value of ideas should be decided on merit, not on the power of the position of the originator. Some ideas will be viewed positively by some and negatively by others. That is part of the process of establishing conjoining conversation. It is important to trust in the collaborative process and thereby allow the combined wisdom of the conjoining conversation to prevail. The whole effort is designed to not only bring the combined wisdom of the group to the generation of solutions to problems, or group-generated action plans to the implementation of strategies for improvement, but, more important in the long term, to develop a partnership of sharing and trust among the stakeholders. For employees, every effort must be made to provide a feeling of job security. For parents, efforts must be made to allay their fears that reprisals may be taken against their children because of the differing views of the parents. It can be surprising to learn the quiet fears and insecurities many of these stakeholders bring to the table regarding the school district. This important point is easy to miss, and can thereby subject the process to failure due to the silence these fears generate. Building principals must learn the skills of active engagement and mutual trust development.

Trust must be generated in order for the conversations of those involved in the strategic process to be effective. Strategic planning produces both a process and a product. The process defines the rules for engagement of the stakeholders, including decision making, selection of representatives, and relationships between the various strategic planning teams and other school-related committees such as the school board. The governing body must be committed to the process. The important commitment on the part of the school board is the sharing of the power of decision making with the stakeholders of the school district. By so doing, they are empowered, in the final analysis, to make more effective decisions. This does not represent a relinquishing of school board decision-making responsibilities. Rather, it represents capitalizing on the opportunity to make better decisions based upon the combined wisdom derived from stakeholders collaboratively involved in the process. Support and commitment of the stakeholders follows. Ultimately, the school board is empowered by the reflection in their decisions of the combined wisdom of the school district stakeholders. Local school districts represent one of the last vestiges of local decision making, and therefore local control, in our nation. The question of who represents a cross section of the school and community is important to the final acceptance of the group decision-making in the process of strategic planning. As much as possible, a planning team should be composed of individual school and community members whose background, experience, and interests reflect a microcosm of the broader school district community in order that the various backgrounds, experiences, and interests of all segments of the school community are represented. School district stakeholders will be committed to final decisions and a decision-making process that they have contributed to developing, either directly or indirectly, through representation.

As the planning team works to develop an analysis of the politics, demographics, mission, objectives, strategies, and strengths and weaknesses of the school district, it is important to communicate its progress on a regular basis to the school community. The written word alone is insufficient to accomplish this important communication task. Gatherings of school community members should be regularly scheduled to afford everybody the opportunity for conversation regarding these matters. These gatherings should be held at the school building level, as building principals are in the best position to communicate with members of their local school community and facilitate the group conversation. The public should be fully and regularly involved. Open conversation regarding the unfolding strategic plan is crucial to the ultimate acceptance and support it will garnish.

BENCHMARKING FOR EXCELLENCE

For years, private sector corporations have recognized excellence by using criteria that reflect the highest performing organizations, in order to bestow upon those who meet these criteria the Baldrige Award for Excellence. In his book *The Baldrige Quality System: The Do-It-Yourself Way to Transform Your Business*, Stephen George delineates these criteria as follows:

Every quality system in every organization—manufacturing, service, nonprofit, government, or education—includes six areas, six of the seven categories in the Baldrige criteria:

1. Leadership

2. Information and Analysis

3. Strategic Quality Planning

4. Human Resource Development and Management

5. Management of Process Quality

6. Customer Focus and Satisfaction

The final category in the Baldrige criteria is 7, Quality and Operational Results, the focus and purpose of all quality system actions (1992, p. 20).

These seven criteria (discussed more fully in Chapter 3) call for a districtwide commitment to self-examination and reflection relative to the degree of quality operational performance in each area of the school district that, according to the Baldrige Criteria, determine excellence.

Benchmarking is tied to both the Five Essentials and the Baldrige Criteria as a means to achieve excellence. In his book *Competitive Intelligence: How to Gather, Analyze, and Use Information to Move Your Business*, Larry Kahaner explains the following: "Competitive intelligence is not just about collecting information. It's about analyzing this information, filtering it, learning what's useful and what's not—and then using it to our benefit" (1996, p. 29).

When we speak of benchmarking, we are referring to two separate but related basic activities: information gathering and the development of intelligence from that information. Public school organizations may take the time and effort to gather information regarding best practices in the field, but that effort alone is not enough. Once the information is gathered, it must be filtered and screened using criteria developed from local school organizational needs. Turning to such areas as represented by the Five Essentials and the Baldrige categories is key to the development of such criteria. The following list represents school district areas where unacceptable results point to topics to be included in the development of this criteria:

1. Governance Program—Standards of excellence are not met. (This is determined by a self-study of each service area of the school district in order to determine compliance with each related standard of excellence. See Chapter 6.)

2. Strategic Plan—Action plans are not complete.

3. Public Engagement—Public engagement programs are not implemented or are implemented unsuccessfully.

4. Baldrige Leadership—Quality improvement principles are not in evidence.

5. Baldrige Information and Analysis—Quality and performance-related data are not utilized in overall planning.

6. Baldrige Human Resources Development and Management—Overall human resource development plans are not aligned with the school district's performance goals.

7. Baldrige Process Management—Systematic processes targeting continual quality improvement and assessment are not in evidence.

8. Baldrige Performance Results—Performance levels and performance trends are not in compliance with standards of excellence.

9. Baldrige Customer Focus and Satisfaction—Requirements of various stakeholders are not being met.

Competitive intelligence within the field of public education should be implemented not because school districts seek to become more competitive within the industry, but rather because it facilitates cooperation and collaboration between school organizations to find, tailor to local needs, and implement a better way of doing business. That business is improving the effectiveness of teaching and the potential for learning.

School district administrative organizations too often are organized as departments or divisions in charge of specific operations of the school district. These divisions (curriculum, business, pupil personnel, etc.) frequently operate in such a way that they are isolated from one another. This generates among school personnel what has been referred to as "silo" thinking—people working in the same departments, meeting with others from the same department, working to accomplish operational targets that have little or nothing to do with the overall mission of the school district, and often subconsciously prioritizing their department's survival above the needs of the district as a whole. For public school sites, the same is true. Secondary schools are often organized by academic departments, and elementary schools are organized by grade levels. Again, like-minded people meet with like-minded people and thereby miss the opportunity to bring the combined wisdom to their discussions that the inclusion of teachers and others with varying backgrounds and areas of expertise would bring.

The same is true regarding faculty meetings where building principals run the meetings by the authority of their position. Most teachers are reluctant to suggest a solution or propose a course of action when to do so would pit their ideas in opposition to those of their boss. Those teachers who are bold enough to do so often have only criticism to offer, with no alternative course of action or solution to propose. The result is that little or no progress on important issues is made, or the principal makes unilateral decisions for which there is minimal faculty support and individual faculty investment.

Rather, in order to create an improved environment for the transformation of schools, we should organize around cross-functional teams that derive their membership from a cross section of academic departments in the secondary schools, and a cross section of grade levels in the elementary schools. In addition, in order to capitalize on this kind of reorganization of our public schools, school principals need to develop the skills of the Five Essentials to be able to facilitate the combined wisdom of all the stakeholders. For school organizations to become all they can be, we must first engage in some "unlearning" about silo thinking and other traditional practices that serve as barriers to the transformation of schools. We need to establish cross-functional teams that include the public, in order to address the problems we find in education today. We should replace the single-mindedness that those with identical expertise bring to the conversation with the combined wisdom of cross-functional teams composed of individuals with differing expertise. The composition of these cross-functional teams will, to some degree, be dictated by the nature of the problem or challenge facing the organization. It is the conversation of a team of individuals composed in this manner that will produce the solutions that reflect high performance of the organization. It is this notion of cross-functional teams that works best as the vehicle to implement a process of benchmarking in public schools.

Although benchmarking in public schools is a system rarely used, it holds much promise as one of the Five Essentials for transforming schools. The merits of benchmarking in the private sector hold true for most of the operations of public schools. In their book, *High Performance Benchmarking: Twenty Steps to Success,* H. James Harrington and James S. Harrington describe, among others, the following benefits of benchmarking (1996, pp. 130–131):

- Integrates the best practices into the organization
- Develops effective measurement systems
- Identifies strengths that the organization can build upon as well as weaknesses that need to be improved
- Has a positive impact on employee pride and morale
- Is an important enabler that helps the organization compete for the Malcolm Baldrige National Quality Award

The transition from private sector application of benchmarking to the implementation of benchmarking in public schools is a relatively easy one. The merits for benchmarking in the public schools are as follows:

- Benchmarking forces the communication between school stakeholders regarding current problems that the Five Essentials can help solve. It provides a major opportunity in the ongoing professional development of teachers. Benchmarking for best teaching practices based upon well-defined student needs often reveals teaching skills and methodologies teachers may need to develop. It aligns staff development programs with student learning needs.

- Because it promotes cross-functional teams, when combined with consensus decision making, benchmarking promotes personal investment in the effort to improve the accomplishment of the school mission.
- In a school environment where change is difficult, benchmarking legitimizes the efforts of the building principal to improve the instructional program and thereby learning.
- It allows for the improvement of the delivery of services without the evaluation of personnel. Improvement is focused on the services produced by the school organization. If the personnel affected by changes implemented as a result of benchmarking are involved in the process, improvement of individual performance is more likely to be another positive outcome of benchmarking.

Throughout this integrated management system, nothing is more important than the quality of human relationships among employees charged with its implementation. Collaboration between the stakeholders of education weaves its way throughout all the essential elements of the transformation of a school.

LEADING COLLABORATIVELY

I recall my first year as a teacher during which I observed Miss Black, a sixth-grade Language Arts teacher. I was very impressed not only with her teaching skills, but also with her almost innate ability to automatically organize for a teaching-learning situation. She was very helpful both to me and to a friend of mine who was also in his first year of teaching. At the end of the school year, it was the practice of the principal to collect lesson plan books from each and every teacher. I remember walking into Miss Black's classroom at the end of the school year to find her using a magic marker to "black out" almost every lesson plan she had developed for the year. When I asked her why she was doing this, her reply was simply, "If I don't do this, others will steal my planning." When I spoke to other faculty members regarding their practice of sharing lesson plans and teaching methods with one another, I found that Miss Black's attitude was rather unanimously held. They viewed teaching within a professional context as competitive and certainly not collaborative. While I'm sure we've come a long way from those days in terms of how we prepare teachers, little is done to develop the requisite skills for team collaboration.

Within a school setting, collaboration is the means to establishing and sustaining a systematic effort that brings together all school stakeholders with the common interest of using their combined wisdom to both solve problems and advance school improvement initiatives using consensus decision making.

Certainly we can all agree that there are problems in public education today, and we all have a stake in them. Collaboration begins with conversation—a collective conversation. Individuals bring different perspectives to a conversation that is enriched by diversity. This conversation should search for solutions. In this manner, we can go beyond individual visions of what is possible.

David Kolb of the Weatherhead School of Management at Case Western Reserve University has studied conversation for many years. He likes to tell the story of conversational practices of the American Indians contrasted with conversations in our civilized world today. One Native American tribe used a simple system of feathers to signal the need for a conversation within the tribe. The individual wishing to speak with his fellow tribesmen would walk to the center of the village carrying a large white feather, which signaled to his fellow tribesmen to gather around and listen to what he had to say. While he spoke, no other member of the tribe engaged in any conversation. Rather, they listened intently to what he had to say. When he had finished, he simply walked to the tribesman from whom he desired a response and handed him a smaller black feather to signal his desire for conversation with this individual. The black feather was passed in this manner from one member of the tribe to another until all conversation was completed (David Kolb, personal communication, Nov. 15, 1995). By contrast, much of our conversation in public institutions today can be best characterized as acrimonious and adversarial. School board meetings would be well served to borrow the simple system of "passing the feather" for engaging in civilized conversation.

The objective of collaboration is to reach consensus regarding the educational solution or initiative that represents the "better thinking" that a combined wisdom approach alone can produce. In this manner, we are able to utilize the combined wisdom of the participants rather than establish singular thought that lacks the advantage of thought building between the participants.

There is a unique dynamic revealed in constructive collaboration. The stakeholders become committed to a common purpose. At the school building level, principals become responsible for facilitating the creation of an environment supportive of personal investment in the process by all the participants. Solutions are revealed through the constructive interaction between stakeholders with different points of view, backgrounds, and social persuasions. Throughout the process, personal investment in decisions emerges. As participants develop a sense of personally impacting decisions, their personal investment assures the assumption of responsibility for future decisions and subsequent actions.

ENGAGING THE PUBLIC

No organization can achieve levels of quality of their product higher than the level of quality reflected by the relationships among the employees and other stakeholders of the organization. For school districts, there is no more important group of stakeholders than their constituents, including students and parents. With this consideration in mind, lessons from the past teach us that we must find a way to meaningfully engage the public in the decision-making process.

Mindless administration of rules and regulations has caused what many would call "public relations problems" for school districts. This manner of administrating a school district may produce consistency over time, but the primary consideration for the school district is whether the educational interests of the students are best being served. Why have schools been under such constant attack from the public? Certainly it is not difficult to see the adversarial relationship that can quickly develop between school administration and the public. A "we, they" mentality can quickly develop, and this mentality has been institutionalized in far too many school districts across our nation. Public engagement offers more than simply an exchange of information. It has the power to gather support and commitment. Public engagement focuses on the meaning and causes underlying problems and concerns. Conversation and dialogue that bring new and commonly understood meaning to old issues are the strengths of public engagement. In his book, *Synchronicity: The Inner Path of Leadership,* Joseph Jaworski (1996) indicates that,

> "The capacity to discover and participate in our unfolding future has more to do with our being—our total orientation of character and consciousness—than with what we do. Leadership is about creating, day by day, a domain in which we and those around us continually deepen our understanding of reality and are able to participate in shaping the future. This, then, is the deeper territory of leadership—collectively 'listening' to what is wanting to emerge in the world, and then having the courage to do what is required" (p. 182).

Strong listening skills are necessary in order to welcome differing views. The requirement for leadership is to become open to new meanings so discovered. The pursuit of such meaning is essential to the development of a collective wisdom on the issues. There is a collective meaning that emerges from sincere engagement that reflects the sum equaling more than its component parts.

STANDARDS-BASED GOVERNANCE AND QUALITY ASSURANCE

In order to be accountable for the quality of education offered in a school district, school boards must adopt and rely upon minimum standards of excellence. These standards should address both the unique needs and the values of the school district. They should also at least reflect minimums required by state standards. In addition, staff and community members should be engaged in their development. As the school board evaluates whether or not the district is accomplishing its mission, compliance with these standards serves as a major determinant. The following school district general areas of service represent the major divisions for standards development:

1. School Board

2. Human Resources and Instructional Services

3. Curricular and Pupil Personnel Services

4. Educational Program Design and Special Education Services

A school district operates on a "governance by standards" basis when the everyday decisions of all the stakeholders, especially the school board, are based on the commitments reflected in the standards of excellence. In this way, collaborative decision making becomes aligned with the school district standards of excellence.

A quality assurance review, commonly used and accepted in both industry and healthcare, provides a school district with a tool for self-evaluation and comparison against internally developed standards. The Standards of Excellence developed for the specific purpose of self-evaluation serve as the objective base for review. The incorporation of quality assurance principles should provide for ongoing strategic planning, as well as restoration and improvement services. A quality assurance advisory committee should be composed of representatives from the community and the professional staff. This advisory committee should review the following issues:

1. The effective delivery of curricula/instructional services as measured against the Standards of Excellence

2. Comprehensive overview of compliance with the Standards of Excellence

3. Procedural revisions necessary for improvement of the Quality Improvement and Restoration Program

4. Annual revision of the Quality Assurance Program

The Quality Assurance Program offers the opportunity to respond to an identified need to bring a particular service area back into compliance with a particular standard. With the Quality Assurance Program, the school board is able to continuously monitor the status of compliance with every district standard. Accordingly, district resources can be redeployed to service areas not in compliance with their standards of excellence. In this manner, district resources can be utilized more effectively where they are most needed. The Quality Assurance Program activates close scrutiny of resource allocation, effective deployment of staff, and meaningful collaboration with community members.

THE INTEGRATED ESSENTIALS

The potential for successful development and implementation of each of the Five Essentials is greatly improved when they are developed in concert with one another. There is no greater opportunity for meaningful public engagement in decision making for a school district than during the strategic planning process. The use of benchmarking and the implementation of an integrated management system such as the Baldrige Management System go hand in hand.

By moving from a traditional decision-making process to a collaborative decision-making model, a school board inures itself to both better decisions, in the interest of students, which are more universally supported, and a decision-making process that incorporates the combined wisdom of the school stakeholders in their decisions. Therefore, as a school board lets go of traditional power decision making, it thereby empowers itself. Governing by standards empowers those involved by deriving those standards from the engagement of the public. Because the implementation of collaborative leadership creates trusting relationships among the stakeholders and because, by design, it solicits meaningful input from the stakeholders, it lends itself well to planning strategically. Planning strategically requires both of these elements to be successfully implemented.

Skill development necessary to acquire and implement the Five Essentials overlaps from one essential to the other (see Figure 1.1). The Five Essentials share a basis of relationship building, achieving excellence, establishing trust, and reaching common meaning and understanding. An organization can achieve a level of performance excellence and quality no greater than the composite quality of the relationships among and between its stakeholders. The Five Essentials facilitate the development of these quality relationships.

THE POWER OF CONSENSUS

Decision making within the organization, as I have described, should be accomplished by consensus that is defined as the absolute agreement of everyone involved in the process. Deciding by majority rule gives rise to lack of support of the decision by the disempowered minority. Working for

Figure 1.1 Integrated Essentials

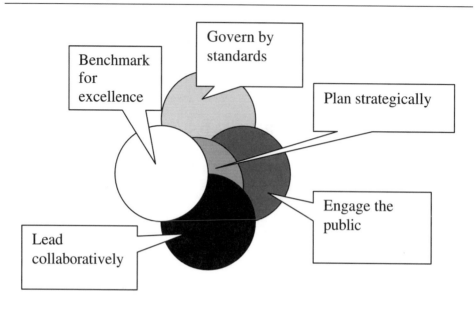

consensus so defined contributes to the development of a collaborative team. The combined wisdom of the entire group gives birth to better decision making. As the group works to reconcile differences, commitment to the ultimate decision is strengthened.

In their book *Primal Leadership: Realizing the Power of Emotional Intelligence,* Daniel Goleman, Richard Boyatzis, and Annie McKee (2002) discuss the role of emotion in leadership as follows:

> In the modern organization, this primordial emotional task—though by now largely invisible—remains foremost among the many jobs of leadership: driving the collective emotions in a positive direction and clearing the smog created by toxic emotions. This task applies to leadership everywhere, from the boardroom to the shop floor. Quite simply, in any human group the leader has maximal power to sway everyone's emotions. If people's emotions are pushed toward the range of enthusiasm, performance can soar; if people are driven toward rancor and anxiety, they will be thrown off stride. (p. 5)

Again, it falls to the building principal to develop the facilitation skills necessary to drive the shared decision making of the collaborative team. The building principal must guide the collective emotion of the group of stakeholders toward enthusiasm for both the ultimate decision and the process employed to arrive at that decision by consensus. The building principal must be adroit in the use of collaborative leadership skills.

Consensus decision making eliminates the "post meeting parking lot meetings" that are inevitable when decisions are made by majority rule. These "parking lot meetings" occur between those of the minority opinion after a discussion has taken place which utilized a majority rule decision-making mentality. The "parking lot meetings" happen because those of the minority opinion have a need to discuss what the majority of the discussion participants were not receptive to considering. The consequences of majority decision making tend to be more political than substantive. Decisions made through a majority decision-making process are devoid of the wisdom that emerges within a consensus decision-making process, wherein those not in absolute agreement with the "majority" thoughts are encouraged to explain their differing notions. Rather than profiting from the inclusion of *all* thinking and allowing the free flow of combined wisdom to produce conclusions not predictable by any one participant, premature conclusions are accepted by a majority vote.

Majority rule in these settings also precludes the personal investment of all participants in the final decisions. Even though consensus thinking and decision making requires more patience and perseverance, the improved wisdom of the final decision as well as the support for both the decision and the process are well worth the effort. Consensus thinking eliminates the need for "parking lot meetings."

RANDOM ACTS OF IMPROVEMENT

In his book, *Insights to Performance Excellence 1999*, Mark L. Blazey (1999) comments,

> Without effective alignment, routine work and acts of improvement can be random and serve to suboptimize organizational performance. . . . Each person, each manager, and each work unit works diligently to achieve goals they believe are important. Each is pulling hard—but not necessarily in ways that ensure performance excellence. This encourages the creation of "fiefdoms" within organizations. With a clear, well communicated strategic plan, it is easier to know when daily work is out of alignment. . . . The strategic plan and accompanying measures make it possible to know when work is not aligned and help employees, including leaders, to know when adjustments are required. A well-deployed and understood strategic plan helps everyone in the organization distinguish between random acts of improvement and aligned improvement. (pp. 93–94)

Most school employees work on an everyday basis in a rather isolated fashion. They may at times work on committees whose purpose is either vague or unstated. The highest performing employees, therefore, develop individual acts of improvement. When viewed in an organizational sense, they appear as random acts of improvement, often with little or no alignment with the organizational goals (see Figure 1.2).

A well-developed and communicated strategic plan facilitates the implementation of individual acts of improvement, which are aligned with the overall organizational plan. Blazey goes on to point out that, "Random acts of improvement give a false sense of accomplishment and rarely benefit the organization" (1999, p. 94). In school districts, there is evidence of this within departments as well as individual classrooms. Without alignment with the organizational goals, these individual initiatives often represent a misdeployment of human and material resources. The organizational effectiveness is not enhanced.

Conversely, when the stakeholders develop and work with processes that are consistent with the accomplishment of goals that are targeted in the strategic plan, the organization becomes much more effective. At the school district level, it is the responsibility of the superintendent to redirect random acts of improvement to align with the district objectives. At the school building level, it is the responsibility of the school principal to redirect random acts of improvement to align with the school objectives. Random acts of improvement must be handled carefully so as to not dampen the enthusiasm of the staff member involved. Principals with collaborative leadership skills are able to direct the energy of school transformation teams to align their decisions with school objectives.

A major goal of high-performing leadership is to create an environment within the organization that creates the possibility for employees to realize personal goals while in the process of attaining the organizational goals. Random acts of improvement can be and many times are counterproductive to the accomplishment of the organizational goals. The Five Essentials help create an aligned environment. With proper involvement, planning, governing, setting standards, engaging the public, and collaborating, we can develop a commitment to a mission which has been impacted on a personal level by the stakeholders of the school or school district. Just as Viktor Frankl in *Man's Search for Meaning* points out, our main concern "is not to gain pleasure to avoid pain but rather to see a meaning . . . in life" (1959, p. 115); so it is with learning organizations. The performance level of members of the organization is directly related to their shared understanding of the meaning of the organization (see Figure 1.3).

SUMMARY

Each of the Five Essentials discussed in this chapter makes its own unique contribution to organizational excellence. At the same time, each of the Five Essentials reinforces and supports the contributions of the others.

Figure 1.2 Random Acts of Improvement and Aligned Acts of Improvement

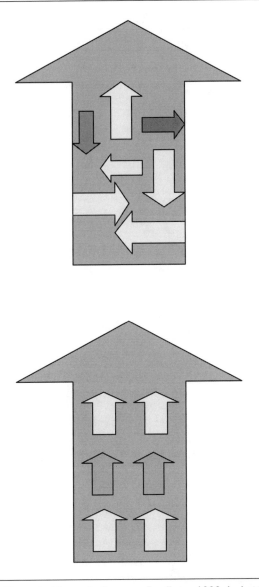

Adapted from Mark L. Blazey, *Insights to Performance Excellence, 1999: An Inside Look at the 1999 Baldrige Award Criteria.* Milwaukee, WI: ASQ Quality Press, 1999, p. 95.

They, by their very nature, are easily integrated into a management system in a natural and flexible manner. This is principally the case because the essence of each of the Five Essentials depends upon common roots in the quality of relationships among and between the stakeholders of the organization. In turn, it is conversation among the stakeholders that reflects the beginnings of ultimate organizational excellence. Within a conversational context, the generation of trust among the stakeholders is the most important determinant of the ultimate effectiveness of the integration of the Five Essentials into organizational transformation.

Strategic planning provides a process for bringing the combined wisdom of the stakeholders to the development and implementation of action plans for the transformation of schools. Benchmarking is a process that brings "best practices" and the filtering of information into usable intelligence to the organization. Collaborative leadership is both the fuel and the lubricant that drives and smoothes the process of implementing the other four essentials. It provides for the formation of meaningful relationships and shared commitments to the meaning and goals of the transformed organization.

It is public engagement that offers the best conduit for school districts to authentically gather otherwise unattainable information from the public and by so doing, garnish commitment to and support for the organization. Governing by standards certainly parallels the process of benchmarking by setting the standards of excellence as the benchmark. Working to comply with locally developed standards of excellence sets the stage for further internal and external benchmarking. Once we locally determine the standards of excellence for the organization, we can institute a well-articulated quality assurance program, which, in concert with a strategic plan, insures that human and material resources are continuously aimed at the attainment of these standards.

Because of their related nature, the potential for successful development and implementation of the Five Essentials is enhanced by their simultaneous development. The skills required by one of the essential processes are related to the skills required by the others. In addition, greater integrity in the implementation process can be achieved when the Five Essentials are implemented in concert with one another.

The component parts of a strategic plan, such as arriving at a mission statement or producing strategies to accomplish the mission, are more effectively developed by applying the skills of the Five Essentials to the process of strategic planning. As part of the strategic planning process, the mission statement should address what is unique about that school organization. What purpose does the organization serve and what are the values and priorities of the school organization? The Five Essentials provide the stakeholders with the skills to more effectively answer these questions. Conversations among the school stakeholders who possess the skills of the Five Essentials produce more accurate answers to these questions and thereby enhance the strategic planning process. As important, the strategic thinking underscoring the mission statement should permeate all discussions and decisions of the school organization. Again, these discussions and decisions produce more effective results when the skills of the Five Essentials are shared by all the participants. The importance of these considerations is echoed in the next chapter.

2

The Power
of Thinking and
Planning Strategically

For a vision of success to have a strong effect on organizational decisions and actions, it must be widely disseminated and discussed, and it must be referred to frequently as a means of determining appropriate responses to the various situations that confront the organization. Only if the vision statement is used as a basis for organizational decision making and action will it have been worth the effort of creating it.

—John M. Bryson (1995)

COMMITMENT BY GOVERNANCE

The commitment to thinking and planning strategically must begin at the governance level. This is not a commitment on the part of the governing body to "do strategic thinking and planning" but rather to become open to the notion that empowerment of the governing body to provide the best learning opportunities for students is maximized by the proactive and productive involvement of all groups affected by its decision making. Too many efforts to develop a strategic plan have fallen short of full implementation at the board

19

Strategic Planning Survey

For each question, indicate which answer best describes your perception of your job situation: Strongly Agree (SA), Agree (A), Disagree (D), or Strongly Disagree (SD).

	SA	A	D	SD
In my school/district, my colleagues and I often share a common perception of future needs and plans.	☐	☐	☐	☐
My individual classroom/department/division planning objectives are aligned with those of the school/district.	☐	☐	☐	☐
In my school/district, we are provided opportunities for discussions regarding future needs.	☐	☐	☐	☐
In my school/district, all employees have a clear understanding of the "vision" of the school/district.	☐	☐	☐	☐
In my school/district, everybody has a chance to become involved in planning for the future.	☐	☐	☐	☐
In my school/district, employees are made aware of changing demographic data.	☐	☐	☐	☐
In my school/district, school district planning has helped me perform my job more effectively.	☐	☐	☐	☐
In my school/district, there is alignment between the allocation of resources and the current long-term plan.	☐	☐	☐	☐
In my school/district, there is alignment between allocation of resources and my needs in my job.	☐	☐	☐	☐
In my school/district, planning is a part of our everyday work responsibility.	☐	☐	☐	☐

of governance level. Many strategic plans are set aside shortly after their adoption because there was not enough time and effort spent with the board of governance for them to make a full commitment to both the strategic planning process and the product. Howard Feddema, in his publication *Internal Coordinator's Guide: A Practical Guide for Developing and Implementing a Strategic Plan from Inside Your School District* (1996), makes clear the importance of communication with the board when he writes, "The Superintendent should be prepared to share . . . organizational change implications with the board when the strategic plan is discussed during the approval process" (p. 129). Time spent achieving this commitment is time well spent. We must build a foundation for collaboration in order to effectively think and plan strategically. In order to better understand the current status of the notion of planning, the Strategic Planning Survey is offered in Figure 2.1.

PREPARING FOR STRATEGIC PLANNING

The commitments involved in building the foundation for collaborative efforts by stakeholders are vital in part because they give a governing body the collaborative power to think and plan strategically. Here is a summary of the activities necessary to ready a school district to think and plan strategically:

- Train the board of governance in the power of thinking and planning strategically

First of all, it is important to decide if the governing board should be trained alone as a group, or if the central leadership team should also be included. This will depend on the quality of local relationships among the individuals involved. The facilitator of the training should be very knowledgeable not only regarding strategic thinking and planning, but also on the subject of collaborative leadership. The format of the workshop should be an informal conversation. At this meeting, it will be important to make certain that the school board understands the concept of realignment of district resources required by strategic planning. Howard Feddema (1996) makes this point clearly when he asserts, "Before a board can be expected to approve a strategic plan, they need to know the budget implications of that plan" (p. 128). The following issues should be openly discussed and related to the local situation:

1. Present the merits of strategic planning and thinking as they relate to the needs of the school district.

2. Discuss the need for commitment from the governing board to the process and what this commitment will mean throughout the development and implementation of a strategic plan.

3. Underscore the relationship strategic planning and thinking have to increased student achievement and increased learning opportunities.

4. Illustrate that the strategic plan becomes the priority for all of the school district. Those involved in "pet projects" will no longer be able to rely on political maneuvering to capture budget dollars for small, vocal interest groups. The strategic plan will direct the budget.

5. Set the stage for full accountability. Discuss how district resources will be directed to accomplish the district mission and how a constant flow of information will continuously update the school community on the accomplishments related to the strategic plan.

   - Develop a plan to engage the stakeholders in the process of thinking and planning strategically

Develop a "road show" to tour the school district in order to hold conversations with the stakeholders regarding the purpose of strategic planning and engagement. These people represent the pool of talent from which the district will draw to help develop and implement the strategic plan. For their engagement in this process to be effective, they must be enthusiastic supporters of strategic planning. Howard Feddema (1996) puts it this way:

> The intended result of this step is to create widespread understanding of what strategic planning is, how it will benefit the district, how it will be developed, and who will be involved in the development of the plan. A second intended result is that there is general awareness, even enthusiasm, that the plan could make a significant positive difference in the school system. (p. 93)

In order to gain their commitment to the process, parents, teachers, administrators, classified staff, and other community members must be given the opportunity to understand the need for and the merits of strategic planning, including collaboration.

From the beginning of this enterprise, the teacher union leadership should be involved in making decisions regarding the "plan to engage the stakeholders." This is the best manner in which to insure their commitment to the process.

- Establish a structure that enables the process of thinking and planning strategically to drive all operations of the school district

During the course of normal, everyday operation of the school district, employees will be faced with decisions on district spending that may or may not contribute to the accomplishment of the district mission. Even though these decisions are not crucial to the accomplishment of a mission that has not yet been adopted by the district (during the development stage of the strategic plan), they become imperative to the integrity of the successful implementation of the plan once it has been adopted. In other words, everyday decisions must align with and be compatible with the school or school district mission.

During the planning process, in-service education for all employees should focus on how the plan will direct the district resources. Howard Feddema (1996) addresses the issue of realignment of job responsibilities in this way:

> It is an unrealistic expectation that a transformational change effort can be shoehorned into the existing organizational structure of a school district. . . . Once you know which action plans are scheduled for next year's implementation, look at the implications

this work will have on how you deploy people within the district. . . . Will anyone assume new responsibilities? If so, what current responsibilities will be abandoned or de-emphasized? (p. 129)

Because everyone will have the opportunity to become involved in the planning process, understanding how the operational function of each person's job responsibility will be realigned to become compatible with the accomplishment of the district mission will help solicit commitment to the process.

- Engage and educate the news media in the process of thinking and planning strategically

The process of strategic planning is time consuming and devoid of overnight sensational decision making. It is therefore very important to take time to explain to the media the need for strategic planning. Furthermore, decisions along the way should be shared with the media on a continual basis.

- Establish stakeholder conversation circles

Prior to the time that the planning team is established, leadership teams composed of board members, administrators, teachers, classified staff, parents, and teacher union leaders should meet throughout the community in conversation circles with members of the community. The purpose of these meetings is to engage in conversation regarding the strategic planning process. Howard Feddema (1996) underscores the importance of these meetings:

Face-to-face communication should be used to supplement and reinforce the written communication. This is usually accomplished with a series of meetings where staff, parents, and other community members can ask questions about the development of a strategic plan. Many people will not believe that the strategic plan is a district priority until they have an opportunity for personal contact with district leaders. We suggest you start with internal publics and then extend communication to various external constituencies of the school system. (p. 94)

Members of the community should be given the opportunity to fully discuss and question the process. These conversation circles will gradually build a momentum of support for and excitement about the planning process. It is essential that these activities be accomplished prior to the implementation of the strategic planning process. If the stakeholders do not understand the power of thinking and planning strategically, there will be strong resistance to it. When you encounter strong resistance to such a powerful tool for the district, you quickly find yourself in the same confrontational "we, they" environment that led you to the need to approach your governance differently in the first place. Many school districts have failed at their attempts at change for this reason.

THE POWER OF CONVERSATION IN PUBLIC EDUCATION

Many administrators and teachers, mostly because of parental demands that they do not know how to meet, become confrontational when asked to perform differently by parents or other stakeholders. Once conversation becomes confrontational, there is little chance for those involved to combine their wisdom to solve a problem or meet a new challenge. Rather, what quickly develops is a series of accusations and charges that have little or no relevance to the problem or challenge at hand.

The power of conversation in public education today is based upon respect for both what others have to say and for the responsibility those involved in the conversation have for the decisions the conversation may yield. In many conversations among stakeholders today, there is not only little or no such respect, there is not even a recognition of the need.

How we speak, the tones and nonverbal messages, is received by the listener as a more legitimate communication than what we say. The first step in productive conversation is to make sure we are communicating our actual intent. The best method for monitoring your own conversation is the response you receive from those with whom you are communicating. We must recognize that it is *conversation* that engages meaningful exchange of ideas—not a monologue. Our goal is to arrive at common meaning through authentic conversation. Many conversations in the public sector today involve the participants discussing ideas with the goal of "winning" the conversation. This, of course, will not move us toward our goal of engaging in dialogue in order to combine our wisdom to arrive at new, more potentially productive meanings, commonly understood. Common understanding is achieved through authentic dialogue. Collaborative conversation rather than competitive discussion brings about commitment not only to the ideas produced through the conversation but, in a cumulative fashion, it fosters commitment to the ultimate vision and therefore goals of the organization.

When stakeholders are engaged in conversation regarding the school district, coherence—making sure we understand each other's meaning—is of paramount importance. Conversations that involve a rephrasing of one another's ideas are most likely to achieve common understandings. We all bring our opinions to the table of conversation. Inherent within these opinions are cultural beliefs, often obtained at an early age. Intransigence concerning these issues is often the most difficult barrier to achieving a collective vision. These are the hard-held beliefs about which we should exercise the most sensitivity.

In order to realize the power of conversation within an organization, it is important to

1. Ponder each other's ideas without judgment.

2. Become sensitized to others' feelings and ideas.

3. Work to arrive at a meaning which is shared.

4. Decide by complete consensus.

When we allow ourselves to converse in this manner, a new form of collective consciousness will follow.

THE POLITICS OF STRATEGIC PLANNING

Strategic planning should be undertaken only when strategic thinking has been adequately communicated with all stakeholders throughout the district. Thinking strategically requires thinking differently, thinking systemically, and basing individual decisions on a thought process that incorporates the achievement of the mission as the major determinant among the factors comprising the decision. Stakeholders thinking strategically infuse their conversation with strategic considerations. Various elements of the organizational mission will be reflected in such conversation. Thinking strategically requires consciously considering how a decision being contemplated contributes to the accomplishment of the organizational mission, until doing so becomes second nature to the stakeholders. Strategic planning will face less resistance once the notion of strategic thinking is well understood by the majority of the stakeholders in the school district.

The politics of strategic planning can be a powerful tool or a counterproductive dimension to the development of an effective strategic plan. Feddema (1996) underscores the importance of communication about the strategic planning process when he writes,

> After the board has authorized the development of a strategic plan, the first step in the process is to confirm commitment and readiness throughout the school district about the project. . . . First is to inform both internal and external publics of the school system about strategic planning. You will want to answer the what, why, who, where, and when questions in order to reduce suspicion about the project. Some staff may be unfamiliar with the idea and suspect that strategic planning is merely another fad which will not

amount to much. You want a sufficient number of people to genuinely be enthusiastic about the promise of strategic planning before you begin. (pp. 92–93)

Who, what, where, when, and how are of primary importance. Who should be directly involved? What are the various roles of the stakeholders? Where should the planning take place? When should the planning take place? How should the decision to commit to strategic planning be made? All of these questions should be answered and communicated to all concerned.

How Should the Decision to Commit to Strategic Planning Be Made?

Without question, deciding to engage in strategic planning represents a major commitment. The school district should not be in a state of crisis of any sort. Feddema (1996) goes on to caution,

Sometimes we suggest waiting if the following situations are occurring:

1. Aftermath of a serious political problem such as a bitter strike, or a messy superintendent crisis.

2. Major commitment to a previous change effort is completely absorbing people. For example, sometimes a major remodeling project should be completed first. (p. 88)

There should not be indicators of major stress within the school district. As suggested by Feddema, school districts recovering from teacher strikes, experiencing strained board superintendent relations, or suffering from staff cutbacks due to financial shortfalls should not embark on strategic planning. The daily operation of the school district should be relatively smooth, albeit in need of improvement. Crisis management does not lend itself to strategic planning. Strategic planning will itself bring some stress to the school district, but it is stress that can be managed toward the productive end of strategic planning.

Clearly, it is the governing body which must early on make its commitment to strategic planning known. This should be done on an individual as well as a collective basis. Commitment from the governing board should reflect a clear understanding of just what their commitment means.

The stakeholders should see the need to plan strategically. Ultimately, it is the opportunity to improve the potential for student achievement that serves as the determinant to committing to strategic planning.

Who Should Be Directly Involved?

The executive leadership team of the school district should take the lead in making decisions regarding the makeup of the district planning team. Care should be taken to involve selfless individuals known for their devotion to students and increased learning opportunities. Each political and geographic section of the school district should be represented. The planning team should be of limited size—no more than 40 community and school representatives—or it may become unwieldy.

What Are the Various Roles of the Stakeholders?

Everyone on the planning team should be on equal footing with no more than the persuasiveness of their dialogue to influence the decision making. Each of the stakeholders has the same role. They are each to bring his or her best thinking to the discussion of what is the best manner in which to maximize learning opportunities for students. Every stakeholder comes to the conversation with different background and understanding, and it is the new knowledge produced by each individual's contribution to the final amalgamation of ideas and thought that produces the power of the final strategic plan.

Where Should the Planning Take Place?

The planning can occur in a number of places, but the planning meetings should happen within the boundaries of the school district. As we now know from the research involving the Nine Factors of Public Engagement (see Chapter 5 in this volume), as presented in the publication *Meaningful Chaos: How People Form Relationships with Public Concerns*, by Richard Harwood, Michael Perry, and William Schmitt (1993), holding planning meetings at mediating institutions such as churches or community rooms will help facilitate the engagement of the public in the process. Wherever the meetings are held, they should be frequent and each planning session should be attended by each and every member of the planning team.

When Should the Planning Take Place?

There is no best time to begin strategic planning. As indicated earlier, the school district should be free of crisis and major stress. The start of the school year may be a good time because of the renewal a new year brings. Feddema (1996) comments on this, saying, "We recommend that the planning cycle be coordinated with the budgeting cycle" (p. 89). Whenever it begins, it should be at a time when properly engaging the public is assured. The beginning of the process should be well thought out and planned on the part of the district leadership.

TRAINING THE STAKEHOLDERS

Training in the Five Essentials should involve all the stakeholders. The magnitude of the organizational transformation required to meet the needs of public educators today is unprecedented. Although there may be no more money to meet these needs, a good strategic plan will point the way to a redeployment of human and material resources to fully tap the potential of the human resources of the school district. In this manner, a school or school district can target, in laser-like fashion, the allocation of resources to develop within their employees the skills necessary to accomplish the mission of public schools today. Left unexamined, the allocation of district resources easily falls prey to the priorities of political pressure groups or the whims and interests of one or two employees.

The need to develop new skills demanded by organizational transformation in public education today is matched only by the need to train other stakeholders such as parents and other community members. Cohort groups of educators and parents should be trained together in order to gain the skills necessary as well as to practice them together. By training together, a common understanding of problems as well as a collaborative plan for solving them may be more easily reached.

Building principals play a unique and important role in strategic planning as the logical choice to become facilitators of the process. Their responsibility is to lead the stakeholders in acquiring the skills necessary for the development of the strategic plan. Most important, it is their responsibility to promote understanding of the strategic plan among stakeholders so as to gain wide acceptance and support for it.

The benefits of choosing building principals to be trained as facilitators for strategic planning are as follows:

- Building principals interface with representatives of all building stakeholders on a daily basis and therefore are known and trusted by a majority of them.
- Building principals work intimately with both the district mission statement and the individual school vision.
- As a group, building principals are in a position to clearly see the merits of strategic planning from the beginning of the process.
- Building principals are in a position to give important feedback to the school board regarding the experience of developing a strategic plan.

The opportunity for face-to-face conversation that building principals experience with their stakeholders contributes greatly to general stakeholder understanding of the merits of strategic planning. Moreover, this conversation becomes richer as building principals develop their strategic planning expertise. In addition, building principals collectively are able to provide comprehensive feedback about the progress of school district strategic planning to the governing body, thereby enabling the governing body to make meaningful "in course" corrections and modifications.

THE MISSION AND BUILDING PRINCIPALS

John M. Bryson (1995) in his book, *Strategic Planning for Public and Nonprofit Organizations*, discusses the organizational mission statement as follows:

> Mission, in other words, clarifies an organization's purpose, or *why* it should be doing what it does; vision clarifies *what* the organization should look like and how it should behave as it fulfills its mission. (p. 67)

The mission of the school district should be developed at the district level with the involvement of the school board and a cross section of district stakeholders. The superintendent of schools should play a key role in assembling and training these stakeholders in accordance with guidelines found under the heading, Preparing for Strategic Planning, in this chapter.

The vision of each school should be developed at the individual building level with the involvement of the building principal and representative stakeholders from the local school community and staff members. The building principal should play a central part in assembling and training these stakeholders in accordance with the direction set by the district mission statement.

How each individual school within a district operates and what its organizational structure looks like can and should vary from school to school in accordance with localized student learning needs. However, how each building operates and what form of organizational structure each building assumes must be in accord with the district mission. Building principals must facilitate stakeholder understanding of and commitment to the mission statement.

Bryson goes on to say,

> Identifying a mission, however, does more than merely justify an organization's existence. . . . An organization's purpose defines the arenas within which the organization will collaborate or compete, and it charts the future course of the organization (at least in a broad outline). Moreover, an important and socially justifiable mission is a source of inspiration to key stakeholders, particularly employees. Indeed, it is doubtful if any organization ever achieved greatness or excellence without a basic consensus among its key stakeholders on an inspiring mission. (p. 27)

The building principal's position is critical to the development of stakeholder commitment to the district mission. Moreover, the building principal is best positioned to facilitate full understanding of the mission and how it impacts the building vision. Only if the building principal collaboratively shares decision making regarding the mission and its impact on the school vision with the building stakeholders will the mission become inspiring to those involved. Just as important, only if the building stakeholders fully understand the impact of the mission on the future course of the school organization will the changes necessary to accomplish the mission be embraced by the stakeholders.

PERSONAL INVESTMENT IN THE PLAN

Douglas McGregor, in his well-known book *The Human Side of Enterprise*, describes the essence of what he refers to as Theory Y as follows: "The central principle which derives from Theory Y is that of integration: the creation of conditions such that the members of the organization can achieve their own goals *best* by directing their efforts toward the success of the enterprise" (1960, p. 49). The message for school organizations is clear. It is the responsibility of school organizations searching for transformational change to create the environment in which it is possible for organizational stakeholders to achieve their personal goals while in the process of accomplishing the institutional mission. This is the best way to bring about a sense of personal investment in the district as well as its strategic plan. Organizations that fail to accomplish this experience disgruntled employees and confrontational community members. Emphasizing the ultimate importance of the quality of the relationships among the stakeholders of an organization, Stephen R. Covey, in his book *Principle-Centered Leadership*, points out that, "Culture is only a manifestation of how people see themselves, their coworkers, and their organizations" (1990a, p. 182). In this sense, a collaborative culture for schools transforming into learning organizations is only as potentially effective as the stakeholders believe it can be. Everyone involved must believe and invest in a collaborative culture.

PUBLIC ENGAGEMENT IN COMMUNICATING THE PLAN

It is important for those involved in developing the plan to participate in communicating it to the community. Once the work of the planning team is finished, meetings should be scheduled to communicate the plan and generate interest in serving on action teams, which will work up the specific action plans that, when completed, will serve to accomplish the mission. These meetings should be scheduled at the building level. Having been trained as strategic planning facilitators, building principals are the key to generating public interest and understanding in strategic planning, as well as a willingness and interest to serve on action teams for strategic planning.

SUMMARY

Thinking strategically marks the beginning of an organization's ability to determine its future. It must therefore permeate the discussions of the stakeholders of the organization. In order to begin strategic planning, key groups must be prepared for the process. In addition, the board of governance must be educated in the merits of strategic planning, both in a general sense and in the specific needs of the particular school district.

Communication about the strategic planning process must take multiple forms with multiple audiences. "Road shows," community conversation circles, engagement of the media, and staff involvement should all be undertaken. The power of collaborative conversation regarding this planning should not be underestimated. The process builds by way of one-on-one conversations and group discussions that build into a momentum of understanding and support. Training of the stakeholders can thereby be accomplished in an atmosphere of clearly and commonly understood organizational needs. This approach provides the best likelihood that there will develop a sense of "personal investment" in the creation of the strategic plan and a sense of ownership in the ultimate result.

Once the strategic plan has been completed and starts to be implemented, it is vital that we begin measuring its effectiveness in multiple ways. Certainly, comparisons with other school districts are a legitimate means to gauge our relative standing in our quest for excellence. Best practices, information and intelligence development, and integrated managements systems are discussed in the next chapter.

3

Benchmark for Excellence Using the Sterling System

The basis of competitive intelligence is knowing the difference between information and intelligence.

—Larry Kahaner (1996)

BENCHMARKING, INTELLIGENCE, AND THE STERLING SYSTEM

In order to establish an acceptable definition of excellence with which to compare organizational performance, it is important to utilize a widely recognized and legitimate set of criteria for doing so. As mentioned in Chapter 1, the Baldrige Quality System has served this purpose in the private sector for many years. Based upon the Baldrige Criteria, The Florida Sterling Council presents their seven criteria in *The 2000 Sterling Criteria for Organizational Performance Excellence* (2000). The Sterling Criteria are recognized nationally for defining a standard for excellence in organizational performance. In addition, the Sterling Council awards of excellence are determined on the basis of principles such as leadership, employee engagement, and customer satisfaction. Because of a focus on common elements, the Sterling System lends itself well to assessing organizations practicing the Five Essentials. The Sterling Criteria, transposed to public education terms, are summarized as follows:

- Leadership—School board members and senior staff articulate values and performance expectations clearly to all. There is a commitment to organizational excellence by the leadership team. Senior leaders establish and support a climate within the organization for employee empowerment and innovation. There is an incentive created for developing a learning organization (p. 7).

- Strategic Planning—There is reflected within the school organization a commitment to long-term quality strategic planning. This commitment is evidenced in the way the organization develops strategic objectives, action plans, and related human and material resource allocations. The organization recognizes the ongoing nature of the strategic planning process (p. 9).

- Customer Focus and Satisfaction—The focus of the organization is student achievement. Customer-driven quality is targeted for increased student achievement. Changing student requirements are responded to rapidly. A system is in place to evaluate and improve the ability of the organization to keep current with customers and utilize this current information to improve services (p. 11).

- Information and Analysis—A system is in place to measure the organization's performance as well as how the organization uses performance data and information relevant to the district mission. The organization utilizes a cost-benefit analysis to help make improvement decisions (p. 13).

- Human Resource Focus—The organizational environment enables employees to develop and utilize their full potential. The organization creates the climate in which it is possible for employees to accomplish their personal goals while in the process of achieving the institutional goals. There is alignment between personal and institutional goals. In this manner, full participation and personal as well as organizational growth are supported (p. 15).

- Process Management—Process management within the organization reflects a customer focus and a priority of improved response time in all areas of service (p. 18).

- Business Results—The organization examines its performance levels and improvement trends in quality and school operational performance. The organization compares its quality and performance levels to those of other schools (p. 22).

In their book *High Performance Benchmarking: 20 Steps to Success,* H. James Harrington and James S. Harrington (1996) define benchmarking as "a systematic way to identify, understand, and creatively evolve superior products, services, designs, equipment, processes, and practices to improve your organization's real performance" (p. 11). While little has been written to apply this notion of benchmarking to the arena of public education, there is much to gain if a school district does so.

Larry Kahaner coined the term *competitive intelligence* to mean, "a systematic program for gathering and analyzing information about your competitors' activities and general business trends to further your own company's goals" (1996, p. 16). However, there is little, if any, research dedicated to the application of competitive intelligence to public school education.

Yet there is much to profit from combining this notion with the other "essential elements" to transforming a school. Are America's public schools in competition with private education? Are they in competition with charter schools quickly springing up all over the country? Certainly these questions can be debated, but there is little question that incorporating benchmarking and the concepts of competitive intelligence into the transformation efforts of a school district can be very profitable in terms of increased student achievement.

We live in an information age—or do we? According to Kahaner, we have moved from the information age to the age of intelligence. Information is based on facts, whereas, Kahaner asserts, "Intelligence, on the other hand, is a collection of information pieces that have been filtered, distilled, and analyzed" (1996, p. 21). Intelligence in this sense is what collaborative leadership needs to bring about collective decision making. Information and intelligence are not the same thing. We have all been overwhelmed by the plethora of information now available, but today in public education, as ironic as it sounds, we seldom take the opportunity to use intelligence. With over 15,000 school districts in our nation today, we should be able to develop a network of "intelligence gathering."

At the building level, building principals can generate unique "information filters," reflecting their individual building's needs relating to learning. Many of the frustrations with information "overload" people experience can be eliminated by filtering out information not pertinent to their needs. In order to facilitate this important filtering function, every school should have on staff a school intelligence officer. This position would provide guidance and direction in the following areas:

- developing information filtering criteria
- application of filtering criteria to a body of collected information
- interpretation of intelligence to specified needs
- monitoring and analyzing student achievement data and applying information filtering criteria to this data

For building principals providing collaborative decision-making leadership, intelligence-driven instructional transformation produces significantly improved student achievement. Traditional practice gives way to the requirements of school transformation. For example, building principals should transform traditional faculty meetings focusing upon committee reports and calendars into a collaboration of process management focusing on student learning and improved student achievement.

New standards of excellence can be set utilizing benchmarking. Harrington and Harrington caution that,

> If you simply adopt another organization's approach or adapt it to your item, you will not obtain the desired results. The reason is that as your future-state solution is being implemented, your benchmarking partner's item is also improving. The "copycat" approach to improvement will keep your organization always in a catch-up mode. This means that all future-state solutions must incorporate what the benchmarking partner is doing today and improve upon it before the future-state solution is implemented. The challenge is not as difficult as you might think. No doubt you would implement almost every project you have undertaken a little differently if you had to do it over. This is your chance to further refine the world-class item, while combining the best points from each organization that you benchmark, to set a new standard of excellence. (1996, p. 25)

The skills of the Five Essentials facilitate the type of benchmarking described by the Harringtons. Moreover, the collaborative efforts driven by internal and external benchmarking only serve to more authentically establish ever improving standards of excellence as well as the processes of achieving them.

STUDENT-RESULTS BENCHMARKING

In our schools today, we are accumulating much information regarding student achievement. However, screening that information by developing selection criteria based on local needs that produce a body of intelligence is not widely practiced. Student-results benchmarking is a process that incorporates internal and external benchmarking of actual learning outcomes along with benchmarking against locally developed standards of excellence. Using the intelligence generated through this process, cross-functional teams develop a "student learning-targeted" design for improved instruction. Integrated management systems designed for student achievement excellence begin with locally developed standards of excellence with which the organization is not currently in compliance.

If we start with requirements of excellence found in the categories of Information and Analysis as well as Process Management from the Sterling Criteria for Organizational Performance Excellence and combine them with benchmark-based intelligence and actual student performance data, we can design a reorganized deployment of our efforts and expertise to better improve student learning. The collaboration required to accomplish this produces new knowledge related to improving student learning as a result of improved instruction.

Figure 3.1 represents the integration of the Five Essentials into a process of continuous improvement of the use of data and information to increase student achievement in a school district. The management of this process is what is missing in many school districts today. The practices involved in this process can be found in private sector enterprises but have been used very little in public schools to date.

Many would argue that the "product" of public schools is an educated citizenry. More specifically, to improve this product, we must improve learning. Learning outcomes (student achievement) represent our immediate measure of success. If we begin with current student actual learning outcomes, we can analyze and manage this data and information through a process of internal and external benchmarking, strategic planning alignment, instructional improvement decision making based on "intelligence," and, finally, student achievement improvement.

A. Actual Learning Outcomes—The actual learning outcomes of students throughout the district constitute the beginning of data-driven decision making. These data may come in the form of statewide standardized test results, locally developed testing results, or national standardized testing. Data analysts collect this data.

B. Internal Benchmarking—The intended learning outcomes found in the local strategic plan serve as a benchmark against which we measure the actual learning outcomes. These data are collected and analyzed by a cross-functional team made up of data analysts, teachers, administrators, instructional supervisors, and parents. Members of this cross-functional team should be familiar with the governance program, including the local standards of excellence. Their responsibility is to analyze and note discrepancies between student performance levels articulated in the standards of excellence and the actual learning outcomes.

C. External Benchmarking—The actual learning outcomes of high-performing schools serve as a benchmark against which we measure the actual learning outcomes of the school district students.

D. Actual Learning Outcomes Alignment—The intended learning outcomes of the strategic plan are compared with the actual learning outcomes to determine the status of the alignment of the two sets of outcomes.

Figure 3.1 Process Management of Data and Information to Improve Student Learning Outcomes

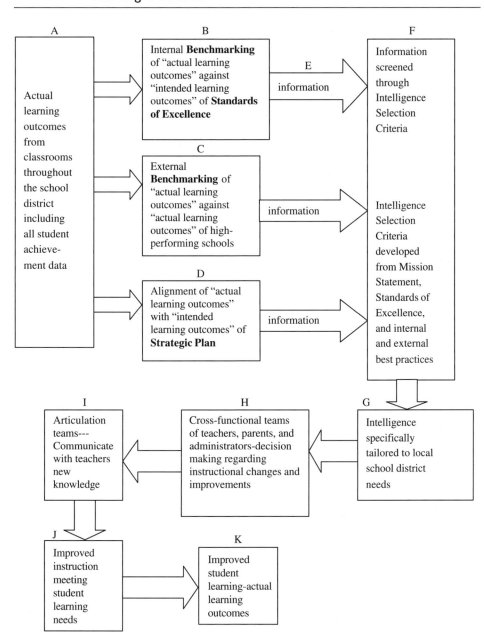

E. Information—All the results of data gathering, comparisons, and analysis (A, B, C, and D in Figure 3.1) are forwarded to the same cross-functional team found in B in Figure 3.1 for information screening.

F. Intelligence Selection—Criteria Development and Information Screening—The intelligence selection criteria are developed from the mission statement, local standards of excellence, and internal as well as external best practices. Once these criteria are developed, the information gathered is screened using the criteria.

G. Intelligence—The results of the information screening represent intelligence specifically tailored to local school district needs.

H. Instructional Analysis Teams—Cross-functional teams of teachers, administrators, parents, and information and instructional specialists collaborate to develop recommendations regarding instructional changes and improvements tailored to the needs of the school district.

I. New Knowledge Communication—Articulation teams of representative stakeholders communicate the new knowledge to teachers.

J. Improved Instruction—Instructional improvements are tailored to meet local student needs.

K. Improved Student Learning—The result of this process is improved student learning.

BENCHMARK FOR ORGANIZATIONAL SUCCESS

The integration of the Five Essentials can be utilized to facilitate a process that emphasizes benchmarking for organizational success, defined as accomplishing the mission. Figure 3.2 illustrates how this process is impacted and managed by the Five Essentials.

Identify Internal Needs

As part of the responsibilities of the strategic planning team, an analysis of strengths and weaknesses of the school district is developed. Just as this analysis of strengths and weaknesses of the school district in general serves as a good starting point for the development of a strategic plan, it also serves as a good beginning for identifying the needs/weaknesses of the instructional/learning programs of the school district. Certainly, ongoing collaborative conversations between the school stakeholders facilitated by the building principal can easily serve as a source for the identification of internal needs. The analysis of weaknesses, found in the analysis of strengths and weaknesses from the strategic planning team, along with collaborative conversations represent just a beginning of understanding the absence or breakdown of processes that can prevent an organization from functioning optimally.

Figure 3.2 Benchmark for Organizational Success

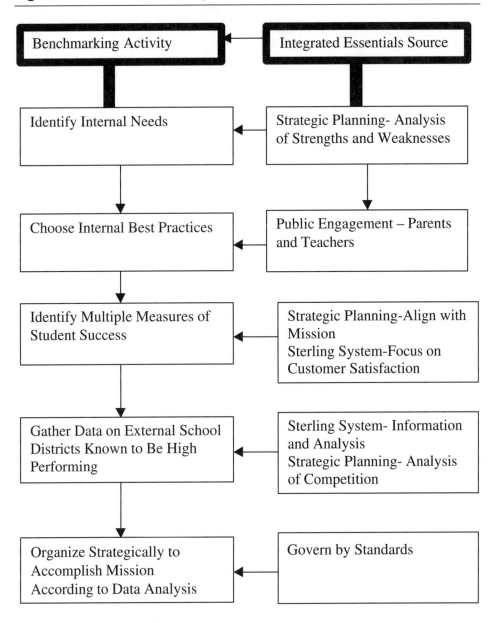

Choose Internal Best Practices

Teachers, administrators, and parents are in a good position to recognize best practices in the classroom as well as in the support areas. The "focus on customer service and satisfaction" category of the Sterling System of Excellence is also very helpful in this enterprise. Best practices from school to school are seldom duplicated, if indeed communicated at all. Within the same school district, internal best practices from individual buildings can easily be identified, shared, and benchmarked by bringing together cross-functional teams of teachers, parents, and administrators representing these different school buildings for the purpose of collaboration.

Identify Multiple Measures of Student Success

This benchmarking activity should go beyond the traditional measures such as grades and state testing. The attitudes of parents and teachers about student success should be surveyed and analyzed in order to discover perceived obstacles and handicaps to increased student achievement. All of the measures should be aligned with the mission of the strategic plan. The involvement of the parents emphasizes the importance, once again, of public engagement in the decision-making process. Again, the "Customer Service and Satisfaction" category from the Sterling System helps provide guidance in this activity.

Gather Data on External School
Districts Known to Be High Performing

The search for high performance need not be limited to other public school districts or schools. Organizational behavior and best practices from external schools as well as from the private sector can be helpful in better understanding deficits in the school district.

Organize Strategically to Accomplish
the Mission According to Data Analysis

If we are going to govern by standards and accomplish our jointly developed district mission, then we must reorganize strategically. Human and material resources must be redeployed in order to maximize the achievement of the organization's potential. This redeployment should be based on two outcomes: the analysis of the benchmarking data and the strategic planning action plans. Job responsibilities must be realigned to reflect the data analysis and the mission of the district.

INTEGRATED MANAGEMENT SYSTEMS DESIGNED FOR STUDENT EXCELLENCE, USING BENCHMARKING AND COMPETITIVE INTELLIGENCE TO ACHIEVE EXCELLENCE

If the organization evaluates itself against self-generated standards of excellence, the Sterling Criteria can help focus categorically which area of

Figure 3.3 Benchmarking Survey

For each question, indicate which answer best describes your perception of your job situation: Strongly Agree (SA), Agree (A), Disagree (D), or Strongly Disagree (SD).

	SA	A	D	SD
There is a system in place to measure the school/district performance internally	☐	☐	☐	☐
There is a system in place to measure the school/district performance externally.	☐	☐	☐	☐
There is a system in place to share school/district best practices across grade levels and school buildings.	☐	☐	☐	☐
There is a system in place to gather data on other schools/districts known to be high performing.	☐	☐	☐	☐
Our school/district has developed and implemented a quality assurance program.	☐	☐	☐	☐
In our school/district, information is gathered, refined, and shared as intelligence useful to the appropriate staff members.	☐	☐	☐	☐
"Intelligence" is a major factor in determining our planning for the future.	☐	☐	☐	☐
Best practices are commonly discussed at school/district faculty meetings.	☐	☐	☐	☐
In our school/district, we always compare our results to external standards to demonstrate improvement.	☐	☐	☐	☐
In our school/district, key benchmark data is used to help formulate the rationale to initiate improvements.	☐	☐	☐	☐

operations needs improvement. This is particularly effective when benchmarking externally and processing benchmarked information internally. Knowledge of the Five Essentials can be employed to bring areas of school district operations into compliance with the district standards of excellence. Figure 3.4 illustrates how the Five Essentials provide the skills necessary to identify areas in the school in need of improvement, filter information to gather intelligence in these areas, align this intelligence with standards of excellence, and thereby propose a plan for improvement.

Figure 3.4 Integrated Essentials

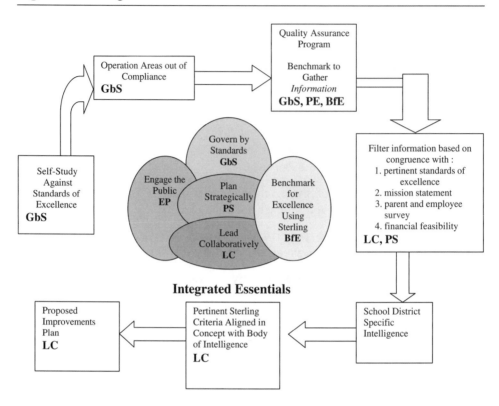

Integrated management systems, which incorporate the concepts reflected in the Five Essentials, offer an ongoing process of improvement. In order to invent and adopt new methods targeted to accomplish excellence in student learning, we must learn to redeploy our human and material resources in new ways. Job descriptions often serve as barriers to this requirement. Just as we are learning new ways to define leadership and organizational development in schools, we must learn to be more fluid in the allocation of our energies and talents as we work to achieve excellence.

Integrated management systems collate the needs of the organization with the talents and abilities of the stakeholders. It therefore becomes extremely important for staff development programs to incorporate the development of skills in the Five Essentials. In this sense, learning how to learn and knowing how to know become highly valued characteristics of school district employees.

SUMMARY

Although used extensively for years in the private sector, benchmarking is probably the "latest arrival" of the Five Essentials to public schools.

However, benchmarking lends itself well to the needs of public schools today. The criteria of the Baldrige Award for Excellence from the private sector also apply well to public education. The Florida Sterling Criteria for Organizational Performance Excellence are discussed in detail in Chapter 7. Benchmarking within the various criteria and core values of these systems, which were developed by studying the characteristics of high performing organizations, offers much promise for the improvement of school organizations.

Through a process of benchmarking and the integration of the other four Essentials, a specific and detailed plan for improvement and ultimate "standard compliance" is tailored to the unique mission and needs of each school or school district. Student-results benchmarking, benchmarking for excellence, and the implementation of integrated management systems require high-performance "process management." Employing the principles of collaborative leadership, which is the subject of the next chapter, best facilitates the attainment of high-performance levels of process management as well as all the other categories of integrated management systems.

4

Lead Collaboratively for Combined Wisdom

Collaboration is the process of shared creation; two or more individuals with complementary skills interacting to create a shared understanding that none had previously possessed or could have come to on their own. Collaboration creates a shared-meaning about a process, a product, or an event.

—Michael Schrage (1995)

TRANSFORMING LEADERSHIP

In their book, *Company of Heroes: The Power of Self-Leadership,* Henry P. Sims Jr. and Charles C. Manz (1996) state, "Now is the time for a new breed of leader. . . . We call this new breed the *SuperLeader:* one who leads others to lead themselves" (p. 4). These authors go on to say, "Under the guidance of a SuperLeader, each individual follower becomes a pillar of strength. An organization with multiple pillars of strength—that is, many competent self-leaders—will not collapse when the leader is absent or gone. The most effective leader, the SuperLeader, helps create followers who are quite capable of carrying on very well through self-leadership. The SuperLeader leads others to lead themselves so that the organization can thrive without constant external direction" (p. 7).

The notion of leaders leading others to lead themselves is consistent with the facilitative responsibilities of collaborative leadership. Tapping the potential of leadership embedded in all stakeholders becomes the most significant contribution of a redefined concept of leadership. However we define leadership, in order to meet the challenge of the 21st century, that definition must recognize the importance of collaboration among the stakeholders in order to tap the leadership ability in us all and, by so doing, maximize the ultimate effectiveness and potential of our organizations.

TRANSFORMING THE PRINCIPALSHIP

Nowhere is the need for a leader leading others to lead more important and obvious than in the school building principalship. Parents are demanding more involvement in decision making that impacts their children; teachers are demanding more involvement in decision making that impacts their classrooms; and members of the community are demanding more involvement in decision making that affects the overall quality of the local educational system. At no time in the history of public education have local and national social forces demanding involvement with schools interacted more closely with the need to improve student-learning opportunities.

Although the need for improving student achievement and the demand for increased stakeholder involvement in schools may be somewhat related, I believe the intersection of these two forces is a reflection of a synchronous occurrence between public schools and modern society. Joseph Jaworski, in his book, *Synchronicity: The Inner Path of Leadership* (1996), explains that, "we've all had those perfect moments, when things come together in an almost unbelievable way, when events that could not be predicted, let alone controlled, remarkably seem to guide us along our path" (p. ix).

The demands for more meaningful involvement of public school stakeholders in their schools and the demands for significantly improved student learning are forces guiding us along a course that requires only the recognition of the need for a transformation of school leadership in order to reveal itself and all the tantamount power to improve both stakeholder involvement and student achievement this transformation can bring. Although this leadership transformation is needed at all levels of school organizations, it is the conversion of the building principal into a collaborative leader that is most important to the ultimate transformation of schools and the related achievement of student learning excellence.

The argument for developing collaborative leadership skills in the building principalship is strengthened by the synchronous occurrence of the demand for increased stakeholder involvement in schools and the demand for significantly improved student achievement. Collaborative leadership practiced by the building principal will only contribute to higher performance in the stakeholders, including student performance, and more meaningful involvement of the stakeholders in the school decision-making process. Conversely, it is precisely the demand for high performance and shared decision making that forms the heart of the need for collaborative leadership.

CHANGE COMES FROM THE EDGE

In order to unleash the power of collaborative leadership, you must continually focus on the goal and then invent the administrative arrangement which accommodates its accomplishment. Administrative arrangements from the past may not accommodate innovative notions that offer the promise of solving today's problems. This is why new organizational structures must be molded and crafted to facilitate new solutions to new as well as old problems. What is required of the collaborative leader is a new mindset that is open and welcomes new ideas.

Collaborative leadership demands a change from the traditional hierarchical organizational practices of the past. It requires

1. An open-minded attitude, receptive to new ideas

2. Respect for colleagues and their opinions

3. Thoughtful consideration of divergent ideas

4. A tolerance for ambiguity that inevitably develops as you work your way through to new solutions

5. Professional ego strength (don't let a traditional "boss" ego or mentality rule your approach

6. Open access for all to all information

7. Patience to listen to others as you work ideas through to a conclusion

Many of our "automatic responses" developed in practicing a traditional leadership style must be overcome. Stephen Covey's notion of "empathic listening" is an important first step. In his book, *The Seven Habits of Highly Effective People,* Covey explains, "Empathic (from *empathy*) listening gets inside another person's frame of reference. You look out through it, you see the world the way they see the world, you understand their paradigm, you understand how they feel" (1990b, p. 240). In order to practice collaborative leadership, building principals must develop the ability to "see the world" the way their stakeholders see it.

Many of the historic and institutionalized administrative arrangements of the past are very difficult to change. In this sense, change must occur at the local level. As Charles Handy indicates in *The Hungry Spirit,*

For the whole to work, the goals of the bits have to gel with the goals of the whole. The blossoming of Vision and Mission statements is one attempt to deal with this, as are campaigns for total quality or excellence. These well-meant initiatives can boomerang, however, if they are imposed from the top. They become the equivalent of the compulsory school song, more mocked than loved. In one organization where I worked, a memorandum was circulated from Head Office stating that with immediate effect the organization was committed to a Theory Y philosophy—a belief that individuals are self-motivating. The contrast between the medium and the message caused hilarity. Like morality, visions and missions are caught, not taught. (1997, pp. 191–192)

All change comes from the edge, not the center. Demonstration of success accomplished through innovative practices that forge new organizational structures begins at the local level. Moreover, it begins with individuals. In schools, it begins with the building principal. It is the school building principal who is in the position to incorporate the advantages of collaboration into his or her leadership as a starting point for the transformation of his or her school.

The following represents initiatives characteristic of the collaborative school principal:

- Encourage the initiation of ideas in conversation with all school stakeholders in both formal and informal conversations.
- Legitimize meaningful parental involvement in decision making affecting students.
- Break down traditional, compartmentalized barriers to collective decision making. Create cross-functional teams representing the various groups of stakeholders.
- Facilitate the natural unfolding of the conversations of stakeholders in order to develop possible solutions to problems.

It is important to understand that the inclusion of parents, teachers, administrators, and community members in the decision making at the school building level must not be viewed as a threat to the legitimate responsibilities of any group of stakeholders. For example, parents should not be involved in decision making at the school level in order to substitute their judgment for the appropriate expertise of teachers. Rather, parents bring feedback and suggestions regarding the impact of school-related decisions that would not be known without the parental involvement. While teachers and parents may have a common understanding of the activities, decisions, and rhythms of the school, teachers, without the inclusion of parents in decision-making conversations, know little regarding the impact at home of decisions made at school. Parents and teachers must understand the role each of them plays in the education of their students. Moreover, it is the building principal's responsibility to provide the support and encouragement necessary for all stakeholders to understand the roles of each other, to be comfortable with their roles, and confident in their responsibilities.

The building principal should avoid the limited potential for worthwhile and innovative decision making that accompanies like-minded groups of decision makers by establishing cross-functional teams made up of a cross section of the stakeholders affected by the decisions made. In this manner, compartmentalized thinking, which does not offer the combined wisdom provided by a wider involvement, is replaced with ideas and solutions rich with potential for improved student learning opportunities.

Some of the requirements of traditional organizational practice in public schools are being suspended to accommodate innovative public school practices. Across the nation, local, regional, and state requirements regarding rules and regulations are being waived, as well as the demands of local union contracts, because they are incompatible with these innovative practices. These waivers are illustrative of the beginning of sweeping change in public school education and organization. They are beginning at the local level—at the edge, not the center.

The relational dynamics of state legislators reflect the politics of compromise, not the characteristics of collaborative leadership. Consequently, public school mandates from state legislatures do not reflect the quality of the restructuring of schools for improved student learning produced by locally practiced collaborative leadership. Change comes from the edge. Those closest to the job know it best. They also know the problems best and, since they do, they are in the best position to use the practice of collaborative leadership to help invent the most effective solutions.

THE ROLE OF PERSONALITY PREFERENCES IN THE RESTRUCTURED ORGANIZATION

In their book, *Type Talk at Work,* Kroeger and Thuesen discuss how the 16 personality types of the Myers-Briggs Type Indicator determine success on the job. Categorizing personality types dates back to the early 1920s in the work of C. J. Jung. It was Jung who first suggested that differences in behavior reflect different preferences found in our personalities. According to Kroeger and Thuesen (1992), "these preferences emerge early in life, forming the foundation of our personalities. Such preferences, said Jung, become the core of our attractions and aversions to people, tasks, and events all life long" (p. 6).

Figure 4.1   Preference Alternatives

Extrovert (E) or Introvert (I)

Sensing (S) or iNtuitive (N)

Thinking (T) or Feeling (F)

Judging (J) or Perceiving (P)

Reprinted with permission from Otto Kroeger and Janet M. Thueson, 1992, p. 12.

Jung's theory of personality was developed into an instrument to categorize these personality preferences by Catherine Briggs and Isabel Briggs Myers. They developed what is known today as the Myers-Briggs Type Indicator instrument. This system has been used extensively to establish an understanding of personality differences. It can be used to greatly increase our understanding of each other as we restructure our organizations. Our goal is to capitalize upon our individual differences in order to more constructively use the talents and abilities of our stakeholders.

All of us have had the experience of listening to a coworker who made absolutely no sense to us. Indeed there are times when those with personality types different from our own sound irrational and sometimes crazy to us. Until we understand personality type indicators, there probably is no reason to believe that the way other people think is right, or even worth listening to. Conversely, those who have the same personality type as us seem to make complete sense as they share their thoughts and ideas on specific subjects. Indeed, we often celebrate same personality types for their lucid thinking. One might even imagine that great progress could be made toward solving organizational problems by putting those with the same personality types to work for the organization. However this is not the case. To fully explore the cafeteria of ideas regarding potential solutions to problems, we must embrace a cross section of personality types. Cross-functional teams are much more effective if we combine various personality types along with a mix of backgrounds.

According to Kroeger and Thuesen (1992), there are four pairs of preference alternatives. They are listed in Figure 4.1. Kroeger and Thuesen (1992, pp. 31, 36, 38, and 42) offer descriptors of the eight categories as presented in Figure 4.2.

There are 16 different personality types, according to the Myers-Briggs Type Indicator. Isabel Briggs Myers, Mary H. McCaulley, Naomi L. Quenk, and Allen L. Hammer point out in their book, *MBTI Manual: A Guide to the*

Figure 4.2 Personality Categories

Extrovert (E) vs. Introvert (I)		Sensors (S) vs. Intuitives (N)	
Sociability	Territorial	Direct	Random
Random	Concentration	Present	Future
Interaction	Limited	Realistic	Conceptual
Multiple	Relationships	Perspiration	Inspiration
Relationships	Energy	Actual	Theoretical
Energy	Conservation	Specific	General
Expenditure	Reflective		
Gregarious	Think, then		
Speak, then	speak		
think			
Thinkers (T) vs. Feelers (F)		Judgers (J) vs. Perceivers (P)	
Objective	Subjective	Resolved	Pending
Firm minded	Tenderhearted	Fixed	Flexible
Just	Humane	Control	Adapt
Analytical	Appreciative	Planned	Open-ended
Detached	Involved	Definite	Tentative
Policy	Social values	Scheduled	Spontaneous

Reprinted with permission from Otto Kroeger and Janet Thueson, 1992, pp. 31, 36, 38, and 42.

Development and Use of the Myers-Briggs Type Indicator, Third Edition, that, "Type tables and type grouping present data on the construct validity of the MTBI—that is, evidence that the MTBI accurately reflects Jung's theory and the constructs it includes" (1998, p. 37). The Myers-Briggs 16 personality types are presented in Figure 4.3.

The complexities of the 16 personality types impact the organization on a daily basis, and simply understanding the differences fosters collaboration. Without understanding these differences, contributions of the various personalities are left to random chance. Personality types in and of themselves are neither good nor bad. However, it is extremely important that we understand that awareness of the interaction of personality types can contribute significantly to the accomplishment of the organizational mission. When staff members are discussing and considering the various options available using a consensus model, all possibilities are more easily incorporated into the group thinking when we understand the differences in personality types. With this understanding, each of us can profit from the other in terms of considering the full impact of our decisions.

Kroeger and Thuesen point out that "one reason so many companies become 'one handed' topologically is the natural tendency to surround

Figure 4.3 Sixteen Personality Types

ISTJ	ISFJ	INFJ	INTJ
ISTP	ISFP	INFP	INTP
ESTP	ESFP	ENFP	ENTP
ESTJ	ESFJ	ENFJ	ENTJ

Reprinted with permission from Myers, McCaulley, Quenk, and Hammer, 1998, p. 36.

oneself with people like oneself. . . . There's no question that while a topologically diverse team may take somewhat longer to accomplish a project, the end result will always be better" (1992, pp. 189–190). And so it is with public school organizations.

Much of the reason that "silos" of isolated departments grow up within the divisions of a school district is that most of these divisions are staffed with similar rather than diverse personality types. According to Kroeger and Thuesen, "within each department or discipline, the individuals involved tend to be type-alike. Those in sales tend to share primarily Extraversion and Feeling. Those in accounting will most likely share Sensing and Thinking. Those in R&D will likely share Intuition and Thinking. The training department is inevitably heavily Intuitive-Feeling. And those in human services tend to be Sensing-Feeling" (1992, p. 192). This creates a perfect environment for the silos to grow more isolated from one another. While one department may desperately need the work product from another department to help accomplish the mission of the school district, the lack of communication and understanding of personality types only serves to stymie the flow of information and increase the isolation between departments.

Conversely Kroeger and Thuesen point out,

There is little doubt in our minds that when different types communicate effectively, the end product can't help but be improved. Extroverts learn better listening skills when they work with Introverts. Introverts learn to speak more freely from Extroverts. Sensors are stretched to see the big picture from Intuitives, and Intuitives are better able to cover details with the collaboration of Sensors. And so on. As a result, if the largely Intuitive-Thinking research department can communicate effectively with the mostly Sensing-Feeling human services department, the end result of the research will likely be more palatable to those for whom it is intended. When we're not aware of this, we tend only to ridicule the other departments because they are so different, rather than recognizing their potential contribution. (1992, p. 193)

In public education today, we have not recognized this very point. Vast quantities of student achievement data are collected and never put to use where they can make a significant difference in how we approach teaching and learning by the curriculum and instruction departments. Understanding personality types and creating sensitivity of one type for another within a school organization creates the environment wherein collaboration can be successful. With this sensitivity, information can be shared productively.

Additionally, and most important, the building principal should understand the impact of personality types. As he or she makes decisions regarding the potential of staff members and other stakeholders, a lack of this understanding can and does lead to unproductive and sometimes counterproductive conclusions and decisions regarding maximizing the contributions of individuals or groups of stakeholders. Most often, building principals hire and assign staff members based on their ability to relate to the "way of thinking" of the staff member or the potential staff member. Like-minded principals tend to hire and assign like-minded staff. This manner of making staffing decisions, over time, can develop narrow and tall "silos of thought."

How much better it would be to hire and assign staff members based on the creation of cross-functional teams of staff members and other stakeholders who think differently. These teams offer a far more effective potential for making decisions that will contribute to the transformation of schools into high-performing organizations.

THE INTERPERSONAL DYNAMICS OF COLLABORATION

Collaborative leadership develops shared meaning and personal commitment. The interpersonal dynamics are as follows:

- Trust is generated between participants by practicing deep listening skills.
- Persuasive skills are developed through the generation of collaborative trust.
- Clarity of meaning and precision of dialogue are fostered.
- The level of problem-solving skills is raised.
- Diverse views and the skills of compatible compromise are fostered.
- Mutually determined commitment to organizational improvement is generated.

Edward E. Lawler, in his book *High Involvement Management*, indicates the following:

Research suggests that participation can affect motivation under certain conditions. Specifically, when people participate in decisions about target performance levels and goals, it can affect their commitment to achieving those goals. It can also affect motivation to produce a high quality product or service when people are given some say in how the work is to be done, what methods are to be used, and how their day-to-day work activities are to be carried out. (1991, p. 31)

Again, the wisdom to incorporate collaborative leadership into the development of a learning organization is underscored. Individuals, given the opportunity to impact decisions affecting their job responsibilities, will make a more sincere commitment to the organizational goals and services. In order for stakeholders to be given this opportunity at the individual school level, building principals must assume the role of collaborative leadership which requires the abandoning of personal power in order to empower stakeholders to make significant contributions to shared decision making.

RETRO PROGRAMS, SACRED COWS

A friend of mine told me a true story about his first four months as a new superintendent of a small suburban school district located in a large metropolitan area. He had decided as part of his entry plan to visit all the schools in the district and spend some time in each school building in conversation with teachers. He made it a practice of asking teachers, "What is the biggest problem facing you currently?"

When he visited the elementary buildings, he found that every single elementary teacher reported that the lunch period created the biggest teaching problem. The lunch period was one and one-half hours long throughout the school district. The teachers reported that almost 100 percent of their students remained at the school for lunch and very few went home. The problem was first a supervisory one and then one of readiness for learning. Elementary children do not require 90 minutes to eat their lunches. These students ate their "brownbag" lunches in less than 20 minutes, after which they were sent to the playground where noontime supervisors watched over them for more than 70 minutes.

When afternoon classes resumed, the students were physically exhausted and therefore not ready for learning. The teachers were very frustrated because they could not get the lunch period shortened. When my friend looked into this problem, he was astonished at what he found. School board meeting minutes revealed that his predecessor had taken a recommendation to shorten the elementary lunch period to the board for approval annually for the previous eight years. In each instance, the board voted the recommendation down. When he looked further into this problem, he found that the length of the elementary lunch period dated back to the 1950s. At that time, the school district bussed every elementary student home for lunch and then bussed them back to school for afternoon classes. To do so required an hour and a half. At the time, most moms were not working outside of the home. They were able to serve their children a "hot lunch."

Well, times had changed but the organization had not. During the same time period that my friend discovered the elementary lunch-period problem, parents were complaining to him that the elementary schools did not serve a hot lunch, as did other schools in the school district. Most of the parents told him that they worked outside the home and there was no way to get a "hot lunch" for their children. It struck him that the problem of the "hot lunches" for the children of working moms and dads overlapped with the problem of teaching exhausted students. The problem for the teachers had become a serious morale issue. It occurred to the superintendent that the solution to these two problems was to offer a hot lunch program at the elementary schools and at the same time shorten the lunch period to 45 minutes.

When he discussed this problem and possible solution with individual school board members, he found disagreement on the board regarding the "mission" of the schools. About half the members felt it was not the job of the school board to feed these children, and they believed that the children should all go home for lunch and supervision.

The final determinant for this new superintendent came with an economic analysis, which revealed that there was an unwritten policy to hire "noon aides" for every 15 students on the playground. This cost the school district $180,000 per year. Because he could provide safe supervision within the confines of the lunchroom with fewer aides, there was an economic incentive to do so. That solved the staffing problem. However, the length of the elementary lunch period was still too long, as it was created in order to meet the demands of a time in our history that had changed dramatically, and the organization had not responded to the new demands of this changed society. At the same time, because of the requirements of a new family reality across America, reflecting either single parents working or both parents working, the customers were demanding a new service in the form of a lunch program for the elementary schools. The two challenges were related. The Problem-Solving Options Table (Figure 4.4) summarizes the components of the best solution for both problems.

Let's analyze just what this new superintendent did in order to discover, define, and solve this problem. In the first instance, he clearly engaged in dialogue with both teachers and parents. These conversations grew into collaboration. If those closest to the job truly know it best, then what he heard was an authentic problem that he collaboratively solved. He solved it by engaging the stakeholders in conversation in which they explained and helped solve the problem.

Figure 4.4 Problem-Solving Options Table

Various Options	Feasibility	Expense	Positive Impact on Other Programs	Acceptance by Stakeholders
Send children home at noon	Low	None	High	Low
Hire more noon aides	High	Hourly @ $12/hr	Low	Low
Shorten lunch period/Start lunch program	**High**	**None**	**Low**	**High**

COLLABORATIVE ORGANIZATIONS

Learning organizations have at their heart collaboration, and collaborative leadership must begin at the top. Stakeholders must be convinced that top leadership is committed to the value of their involvement in a meaningful way. The first step in the process of developing a collaborative organization must therefore be taken by current management.

That first step must be more than just reorganizing. Collaborative organizations must reflect on thinking differently about how they organize to best deliver their services. Craig H. Hickman, in his book *Mind of a Manager, Soul of a Leader*, asserts that,

> Leaders see change as an opportunity to *rethink* what's going on inside and outside the organization. While their rethinking may lead to reorganization, it involves much more than this because leaders want to get to real needs, and this means digging beneath the surface. This usually takes more time, and sometimes the organization must move quickly to adapt to change and therefore may not enjoy the luxury of rethinking. However, leaders would answer that every organization, no matter what the circumstances, must take time to rethink. (1990, p. 174)

The skills of the Five Essentials empower the organization to collaborate in a conjoined conversation that reflects strategic thinking. Strategies, objectives, and action plans set the direction for strategically moving from a traditional form of organization to a collaborative one. For an organization in transition from a traditional form of management to one of collaboration, there are no more important considerations than engaging the stakeholders in decision making and at the same time training them in the skills of the Five Essentials.

ORGANIZATIONAL CHARACTERISTICS OF A PROFESSIONAL BUREAUCRACY

The problem with a bureaucracy is that it does not, by design, provide for nor support collaboration. A professional bureaucracy relies on firmly defined roles whose boundaries are inflexibly drawn. The opportunity for collaboration is precluded. Because the power is positional, individuals tend to work more independently. Gregory P. Smith, in his book entitled *The New Leader: Bringing Creativity and Innovation to the Workplace*, discusses the symptoms of a bureaucracy:

1. A Regulatory-Based Culture, Not A People-Based Culture.

   . . . An organization with no rules would be irresponsible. On the other hand, an overregulated environment hurts initiative and individual creativity.

2. Centralized Decision Making.

   . . . Many times this centralized decision-making process creates additional problems. When you have to climb a mountain for a decision, people decide it is easier to avoid the climb all together. People would rather ignore important issues than fight the system. The result is an organization paralyzed by its own ineffectiveness.

3. Difficulty in Fixing Mistakes.

   . . . In a bureaucratic organization, the people at the top of the organization have the responsibility for interpreting and approving any changes to regulations. This slows decision making because the responsibility and power to make decisions is taken away from those who need it the most.

4. Resists Change.

   . . . Bureaucracies are compartmentalized, and functionally aligned, department by department. The people within the departments have specialized job descriptions focusing on narrow subject areas. Because of this specialization, change becomes difficult.

5. Defined Pecking Orders.

   . . . In its worst form, a bureaucracy almost becomes a caste system. Hierarchical layering dictates what roles to take, who to talk to, and who to associate with. For an organization wanting innovation, this is a major impediment. (1997, pp. 57–61)

Smith goes on to point out,

The traditional view of bureaucracy is a management system based on control and designed upon a hierarchical structure. In the broader sense, the traditional bureaucracy goes beyond just a hierarchical management structure. The negative aspects are far more serious than most people realize.

Bureaucracy affects peoples' thinking. It becomes a top-down mental attitude approach of doing business. This bureaucratic attitude is harmful, and it can become a debilitating disease. It limits peoples' ideas and innate potential. It can rob pride from people, treating workers as if they are incapable of thinking and unable to make decisions. (1997, p. 56)

Without question, traditional bureaucracies stymie the very qualities needed in the stakeholders of organizations today. Innovation, interpersonal interactions, and the invitation to individual commitment are as absent in bureaucracies as they are replete in learning organizations.

AT THE CORE OF COLLABORATIVE SUCCESS

Michael Schrage in his book, *No More Teams, Mastering the Dynamics of Creative Collaboration*, addresses the need that collaboration fills when he notes that:

Collaboration is a *purposive* relationship. At the very heart of collaboration is a desire or need to

- solve a problem,
- create, or
- discover something (1995, p. 29)

Schrage goes on to explain formal and informal collaborations:

Formal collaborations can involve structures and processes (like meetings and new-product reviews); informal collaborations can involve instances and episodes (like scribbling on a napkin over lunch at the cafeteria). The thing these collaborations have in common is people who realize that they can't do it all by themselves. They need insights, comments, questions, and ideas from others. They accept and respect the fact that other perspectives can add value to their own. (1995, p. 33)

Only through collaboration can we create and sustain the feeling on the part of participants that what they felt, what they believed, what they said had an impact on the final product of the collaboration. Only through collaboration can we create and sustain commitment of the participants to the final product of the collaboration. The final product of any true collaboration is the shared creation of the combined wisdom of those collaborating to produce it in the first place.

LEADERSHIP AND FOLLOWERSHIP

Within the organization, the relationship between leadership and followership is critical to maximizing effectiveness. The following indicators reflect an effective collaborative organization:

- Collaboration works effectively to accomplish the mission of the organization when the proper combination of leadership and followership are mixed at the appropriate levels of the organization.
- Those impacted by changes in responsibility are first consulted for meaningful input.
- Collaboration is a function of leadership and followership.
- The ability of the employees of the organization to reflect those characteristics, representative of the best of leadership and followership as the situation requires, defines the total effective collaboration level for the organization.
- For individuals, the relationship between leadership and followership is an inverse one. There is a cumulative and organizationally productive effect of each stakeholder developing their leadership and followership skills, one in concert with the other.

In order to better understand the current status of the notion of collaborative leadership, the Collaborative Leadership Survey is offered in Figure 4.5 (Followership is discussed more fully later in this chapter).

LEADERSHIP NEEDED TODAY

John C. Maxwell points out, in his book *The 21 Indispensable Qualities of a Leader*, that, "The ability to work with people and develop relationships is absolutely indispensable to effective leadership. . . . People truly do want to go along with people they get along with. And while someone can have

Collaborative Leadership Survey

For each question, indicate which answer describes your perception of your job situation, Strongly Agree (SA), Agree (A), Disagree (D), or Strongly Disagree (SD).

	SA	A	D	SD
In my school/district, I have the feeling of shared power with my supervisor.	☐	☐	☐	☐
In my school/district, all information pertinent to a topic of discussion is shared.	☐	☐	☐	☐
In my school/district, there is a pervasive climate of trust.	☐	☐	☐	☐
In my school/district, we are encouraged to take risks and learn from our mistakes.	☐	☐	☐	☐
In my school/district, we are constantly challenged to "stretch" and "grow."	☐	☐	☐	☐
In my school/district, we always use cross-functional teams composed of members with a variety of expertise.	☐	☐	☐	☐
In my school/district, there is an absence of "power struggles."	☐	☐	☐	☐
In my school/district, we approach a problem by first collaboratively defining it.	☐	☐	☐	☐
In my school/district, we practice the principles of collaboration.	☐	☐	☐	☐
In my school/district, I am called upon to offer my expertise when decisions are made.	☐	☐	☐	☐

people skills and not be a good leader, he cannot be a good leader without people skills" (1999, p. 106). Good people skills are required to develop an organization reflective of stakeholder collaboration. Collaboration and public engagement training offer the means for people to reach out to one another. The quality of the relationships between the stakeholders of the organization must be the highest priority for today's leadership.

Leadership is a function of learning—continuous learning. The leadership required today must meet the needs of a learning organization. The stakeholders of this organization must be able to learn from one another. Being proactive regarding searching for innovative solutions is a basic requirement for organizational leadership today.

PRINCIPLES GOVERNING
A PRINCIPAL'S WORK

In order to benefit from the attributes of collaborative leadership, building principals should adhere to the following operating principles:

Be willing to innovate and learn from the consequences that may follow instead of fearing them. We learn more from our mistakes than from our successes. If there is no encouragement to take calculated risks, then the potential for high individual performance will never be realized. And without this potential being achieved, the goals for the organization will not be realized either. Building principals must exhibit professional ego strength and confidence. A fear of failure can be crippling to the achievement of a high-performing school.

Discuss the organizational mission and invite personal investment on a daily basis. Creating the environment in which individuals can achieve their personal goals while in the process of achieving the organizational goals will set a positive tone for the future. Building principals must develop a supportive atmosphere within their school in which staff members and other stakeholders feel comfortable enough to generate enthusiasm for the accomplishment of both personal and organizational goals.

Invite others to help develop an organizational mission by providing the opportunity for them to accomplish their own personal goals in the process. Inviting the stakeholders to invest and commit on a personal level allows them to make an impact on the organizational mission. In this manner, commitment to the organizational goals on the part of the stakeholders is solidified. Principals must make it clear that the contribution of staff members to both the development and accomplishment of the mission is authentically valued and necessary for organizational success.

Facilitate the development of collaborative leadership and thereby promote organizational trust among the stakeholders. Nothing replaces the value of trust in the ultimate success of the organization. Positional power must be abandoned by those who possess it in order to achieve the trust of authentic collaboration. Principals must demonstrate the sharing of positional power by facilitating group decision making and underscoring his or her commitment to the combined wisdom of cross-functional teams.

Combine the wisdom of stakeholders by fully engaging them in organizational decision making. A learning organization becomes highly effective when shared decision making enables the collaborative team to maximize the realization of its potential. Building principals must share responsibility for all significant decision making with their staff in order to effectively engage them.

Solidify trust within the organization by practicing leadership consistent with the organizational mission. Leadership requires consistent mindfulness of the need for others to observe that there is congruency between what you say and what you do regarding the organizational mission. To be trusted, you must trust. Once trust is firmly established, all other dimensions of a learning organization more easily fall into place. Building principals must consistently address the mission of the district and the vision of the school when facilitating discussions regarding problems and challenges of the educational program.

Senior leaders, including principals, must ring true and authentic with their stakeholders. They set the tone for collaboration within the organization by example. Stephen George describes these responsibilities, in his book *The Baldrige Quality System*, as follows:

> Baldrige Award–winning senior executives "walk the talk." They spend the time learning what quality means and how it can be achieved, then train those who report to them, beginning a cycle that reaches everyone in the company. They establish goals, objectives, and measures. They participate in cross-functional teams formed to improve quality in a particular process or area. They meet frequently with customers, suppliers, and employees. They break down the barriers that set them apart from their coworkers, inviting everyone to work together toward a common goal. (1992, p. 61)

Tolerate ambiguity. In diversity, there is strength. The talents and abilities of the stakeholders of a learning organization are its greatest assets. However, without the confidence to overcome their fears and anxieties about their perceived weaknesses, most stakeholders will choose not to take the risk required to engage openly in collaborative dialogue regarding challenges and problems confronting the organization.

When people are not sure or comfortable in group discussions, they tend to withdraw from any but the safest areas of engagement. To do otherwise causes too much ambiguity and the accompanying discomfort. Yet, it is these avoided areas of discussion that must be addressed to solve the problems facing organizations today. It is incumbent upon the building principal to create a comfort zone for all involved to freely discuss even the most potentially controversial issues. The principal should do so by freely admitting to his or her own discomfort when discussing certain issues and problems. Openness and candor are strong signals reflecting the genuine commitment of the building principal to collaborative leadership, and they serve as a compelling invitation for others to follow his or her example.

Overcoming fear of failure. The culture of the organization is a major determinant in creating a "safe comfort zone" for stakeholders in the organization to engage in discussions reflecting a wide diversity of opinions and experiences. Senior management has the responsibility to set the tone for a "risk-free" collaborative environment within the organization that encourages the combined and best thinking of the stakeholders. In order to capitalize on the strength of the differences between people, the following guidelines are helpful:

1. Create an informal opportunity on a regular basis for stakeholders to get to know each other. Sharing their personal goals, interests, and hobbies often helps break down barriers created by not knowing each other.

2. Take every opportunity to eliminate a competitive environment between individuals, departments, and schools. Sharing the work product of the Five Essentials (e.g., benchmarking data) between individuals, departments, and schools generates collaborative relationships that empower the organization to become more effective.

3. Use cross-functional teams to help eliminate a "bunker mentality" encased within "silos of silence" throughout the organization. Again, as these teams are formed, stakeholders involved should be afforded opportunities to get to know one another on an informal basis.

4. Replace the "top-down" bureaucratic hierarchy with collaborative leadership and a commonly developed purpose of the organization.

5. Establish a common purpose for the organization understood by all the stakeholders. With the underlying purpose shared by all, individuality and creativity are encouraged. Creative differences are more productive when grounded by common purpose.

6. Treat perceptual differences with respect. These differences will produce a more effective result for the organization. When encouraged and comfortable, individuals will produce a deeper meaning to understanding the problem or challenge. They will also produce a more significant contribution to the resolution of the problem.

LEGITIMATE FOLLOWERSHIP

In the movie *Gandhi*, Mahatma Gandhi leads a group of demonstrators, only to confront mounted police riding at full gallop toward them. Not knowing what to do, he looks around for help. One of the demonstrators, evidently a horseman, proclaims that they should all lie down. "The horses will not step on us if we lie down," he shouts. Immediately, Gandhi repeats the declaration and motions with his arms that everybody should lie down. Was this situational leadership or was it followership? Did

Figure 4.6 Collaborative Leadership and Discerning Followership

Collaborative Leadership	Discerning Followership
Facilitates the development of organizational vision	Actively seeks clarity of the organizational vision
Involves stakeholders in decision making	Actively promotes institutional value found in mission
Actively seeks feedback on organizational performance	Asks critical questions relative to accomplishment of mission
Listens deeply	Volunteers individual expertise
Incorporates combined wisdom into decision making	Monitors others'adherence to the mission
Makes personal commitment to mission accomplishment	Takes initiative to help accomplish mission

Gandhi become a follower because he did not know what to do, or was it just wise leadership that allowed him to follow the advice of somebody more knowledgeable on this issue than himself?

Robert W. Terry, in his book entitled *Authentic Leadership,* points out that, "Some people do not like the term [follower] because they find it suggests passive, almost robot-like adherents who exhibit nonreflective obedience" (1993, p. 214). I'm sure most of us share some of this feeling. After all, we have not been taught as Americans to "just follow." However, under closer consideration, discerning followership reveals itself to be crucial to the achievement of organizational excellence.

The relationship between leading and following is very important to the accomplishment of the mission and the overall success of the school or school district. Figure 4.6 presents characteristics of collaborative leadership and discerning followership:

Followership within an organization is indeed no less important than leadership. Each stakeholder must provide both leadership and followership in order to accomplish the mission. Just as with Gandhi when confronted with galloping horses, different situations call for various combinations of leading and following from various stakeholders.

Relationship Between Leading and Following

The clearer the goal, the easier it is for followers and leaders to achieve it. The relationship between leading and following is a complementary one. An effective organization needs quality followership as well as leadership. According to Robert Terry, "Lack of creative engagement is the opposite of both leadership and followership" (1993, p. 216). The crucial element common to both is active engagement of stakeholders.

Thomas J. Sergiovanni, in his book *Moral Leadership: Getting to the Heart of School Improvement*, distinguishes between leaders and followers in this way:

> Followers are people committed to purposes, a cause, and a vision of what the school is and can become, beliefs about teaching and learning, values and standards to which they adhere, and convictions. . . . In other words, followership requires an emotional commitment to a set of ideas. (1992, p. 71)

There is an emotional dimension to the personal investment followers make to a collaborative organization. Collaborative leadership easily facilitates this personal investment. Sergiovanni goes on to say,

> When followership and leadership are joined, the traditional hierarchy of the school is upset. . . . Further, a transformation takes place, and emphasis shifts from bureaucratic, psychological, and technical-rational authority to professional and moral authority. As a result, hierarchical position and personality are not enough to earn one the mantle of leader. Instead, it comes through one's demonstrated devotion and success as a follower. The true leader is the one who follows first. (1992, p. 72)

In this sense, leading and following are less the basis for positions and jobs and more the reflections of a mindset driven by emotional commitment to a commonly developed vision. All of us are leaders and followers in various proportions according to various situations. Sometimes leading is following, and other times following is leading.

LOCAL LEADERSHIP ACADEMY

Education in the 21st century will face challenges that will require adapting to advanced technological changes, global focus, privatization, diversity, and changing demographics. To meet these challenges, educational organizations must become collaborative with their shareholders. This requires different administrative leadership skills than those that have served public school educators in the past. Educators of the 21st century will have to adjust to the ever-changing needs of students in this technological and global society. Teachers in a collaborative, site-based organization will need leadership skills as well. Parent and community stakeholders must also have leadership and collaborative skills in order to be productive shareholders in the educational process.

Human resource development serves as the cornerstone for change in the transformation to learning organizations. It is an ongoing process that draws its curriculum from the needs established by the application of the skills of the Five Essentials. The stakeholders should be trained together in order to further advance the spirit of collaboration. Teachers, parents, and administrators should be trained in cohort groups of 30 to 40 participants. Local leadership academies should be established to offer educational community shareholders an array of leadership training opportunities. Cohort groups representing community members, parents, teachers, administrators, and school board members would profit greatly from this opportunity. The following seminars and workshop series are examples of the types of learning opportunities that can be offered:

The Leadership Series

The Leadership Series focuses on training in the skills of leadership, followership, and collaboration. Personality types and adult learning skills, as well as high-performance characteristics, are identified, assessed, and developed. Over the course of nine days throughout the school year, collaboration skills are learned in team settings that have a direct and positive impact on the various stakeholder involvements in the school or school district.

Collaboration for Successful Schools

In this two-day seminar, collaboration training builds on self-understanding of the participant to the benefit of achieving team goals. Leadership and followership are studied in the context of achieving personal goals while in the process of achieving those of the school or school district.

Public School Governance

The participants are taught how to build standards of excellence in each of the service areas of their school or school district in a manner that is reflective of individual school or school district values and needs. The skills required to complete self-studies and validation of self-studies in each school or school district service area are taught and practiced. Quality assurance programming that reflects collaborative leadership finishes off this seminar series.

Strategic and Competitive Planning

The principles of strategic planning are integrated with the private sector concept of "competitive intelligence" in order to prepare the leadership of the school or school district to employ the skills necessary to transform it into a high-performing organization. Participants are taught the methods of utilizing and developing human and material resources of the school or school district in order to maximize learning potential for students, K-12.

Resolving Conflict in Public Issues

Participants are trained in principles of conflict management and collaborative leadership including, but not limited to, ethnic diversity, values education, special interest groups, proper roles of stakeholders, and student management. Issues facing the participants in their roles are used in scenarios for practical applications and resolving conflicts such as differing parental expectations, concern over discipline and safety, disputes between labor and management, and taxpayer revolts.

Reframing Educational Organizations

Participants are instructed in the principles of managing change in a public school setting. Utilizing the Five Essentials, participants apply these principles to their role in reframing their school or school district in order to transform their organization into one of high performance. Building attitudes receptive to change and skill development relative to implementing change are examined.

Leadership in Learning and Knowing

Leadership skill training is mixed with the current research on learning and knowing in nontraditional educational systems. "Learning how to learn" and "knowing how to know" are presented in relation to major elements for reframing leadership in the 21st century.

Quality Challenge in the Public Sector

Utilizing a quality challenge designed for educational institutions, participants learn how to apply quality standards to the classroom, the school building, and the school district. The Baldrige Quality System is adapted to public schools. Such areas as benchmarking, customer satisfaction, and management of a quality process are studied and applied to the public education sector.

Systems Thinking and the Learning Organization

Participants apply systems thinking (see p. 68, this volume) to the development of a strategic plan to transform schools into high-performing organizations. In addition, participants learn how the application of systems thinking and strategic planning facilitates the development of a learning organization. Structuring schools or school districts to assure quality processing of information in order to learn, grow, and flourish is emphasized.

Figure 4.7 Environmental Leadership Perception Inventory

For each question, indicate which answer describes your perception of your job situation, Strongly Agree (SA), Agree (A), Disagree (D), or Strongly Disagree (SD).

In my present position within my organization I:	SA	A	D	SD
Can take any reasonable initiative I choose.	☐	☐	☐	☐
Am supervised in a proactive, supportive manner.	☐	☐	☐	☐
Am encouraged to be innovative and creative in the delivery of educational services to children.	☐	☐	☐	☐
Am supervised in a fair-minded manner.	☐	☐	☐	☐
Am supervised in a manner that encourages me to work harder.	☐	☐	☐	☐
Feel I am a meaningful part of organizational accomplishments.	☐	☐	☐	☐
Am able to make a meaningful impact on decisions that change my role within the organization.	☐	☐	☐	☐
Feel my ideas will be given fair and careful consideration.	☐	☐	☐	☐
Collaborate openly and freely with all my working colleagues.	☐	☐	☐	☐
Meet on a regular basis with my colleagues in order to problem solve.	☐	☐	☐	☐
Receive a steady flow of communication regarding the progress of my organization.	☐	☐	☐	☐
Feel free to express my ideas without unfair judgment or reprisal.	☐	☐	☐	☐
Am given the in-service opportunities I need.	☐	☐	☐	☐

Creating a Learning School

Utilizing principles of the development of a learning organization, participants learn how to apply these principles to the everyday practice of teaching and learning in classrooms, individual schools, and school districts. In addition, participants will learn about the latest research regarding student and adult learning.

For many of these leadership development seminars, it is important to measure the participant's perception of their leadership environment.

Administering the Environmental Leadership Perception Inventory (see Figure 4.7) helps establish an indication of where an organization falls on the learning organization scale.

SYSTEMS THINKING

It is important to note that systems thinking should be used to evaluate the delivery of educational services. Evaluation of the delivery of educational services should be accomplished separate and apart form the evaluation of the individuals involved. Often, correcting the delivery of service problem will empower the individual to perform at a more effective level. Have you ever heard, "With the system broken, how do you expect me to get my job done?"

Thinking systemically goes hand-in-hand with collaborative leadership. As Phillip Schlechty, in his book *Inventing Better Schools*, points out:

> Those who would change school systems must think systemically. They must first believe that the way systems are put together shapes and molds how men and women behave in them. This is not a deterministic view, nor does it deny the importance of the individual in human systems. Men and women create systems, and they can destroy or modify them.
>
> Furthermore, as Peter Drucker has observed, real change in an organization is always started by some individual, and the greater the change, the more likely that person is to be a "monomaniac with a mission" . . . [G]reat leaders are needed if real change is to occur. (1997, p. 185)

Far too many decisions in schools today are made in isolation from those stakeholders the decision will affect. Without systems thinking, random acts of improvement may or may not align with the mission of the organization. Collaborative leadership fosters systems thinking by bringing to the table of decision making a detailed and comprehensive discussion of all the facets of a new initiative or proposed solution to a problem. How decisions impact the total organization is fully discussed through the collaboration of the stakeholders.

In today's climate, decisions at individual schools can easily be made without consideration of the impact of that decision on the larger school district. Indeed, the "School-Based Management" movement can be interpreted as promoting independent decision making. However, the effectiveness of decision making at the individual building level or across a school district is only enhanced by the collaboration of all the stakeholders.

The sky is the limit when we put into full implementation the power of collaborative leadership that creates the environment in which organizational stakeholders can make their best contribution to the overall effectiveness of the organization, best measured by how well the organization maximizes student learning. In their book *The Dance of Change*, Peter Senge et al. reflect this sentiment:

> Who knows how much of the reflective genius of organizational members is never applied within their workplace? This is an immense loss for them as individuals and for our organizations. It is probably one of the primary reasons that most change initiatives remain superficial and profound change is so rare. (1999, p. 199)

Superficial change is as safe as it is ineffective. If there is a history within a school district of dire consequences for individuals who take initiatives that miss the mark, then you can be sure that there will be little incentive for the stakeholders to share their best thinking because its potential impact is untested and unknown. On the other hand, if there is a history of experiencing failure and learning to regroup and learn a better way from that failure, then the incentive to establish and maintain a momentum of initiating improvements through change will become firmly established within the organization. Only then will the organization become ready to sustain profound change.

SUMMARY

In schools today, transformation comes from an environment that is supportive of change and innovation. In contrast to traditional hierarchical structures, our schools today require the development of trust characterized by support of risk-taking and collaboration. Collaborative leadership avails us of the opportunity to benefit our organizations with the combined wisdom of all the stakeholders, which would otherwise be easily passed over. Most important, collaborative leadership develops, on the part of the stakeholders, shared meaning of the organization and personal commitment to its goals.

As we study the individual relationships among the organizational stakeholders, it is helpful to understand the meaning and impact of various personality types. Simply understanding the existence of sixteen various personality types fosters collaboration. The complexities of these personality types impact the quality of relationships and decision making within an organization on a daily basis. With the understanding of the impact of personality type within the organization, we can far more readily come to an understanding of what it means to share power in a non-threatening, supportive manner.

By way of contrast, professional bureaucracies rely on firmly defined roles and boundaries that do not provide the flexibility required by the demands of a changing world around us. Leaders today must develop a mindset that is open to innovations, experimentation with new organizational forms, and full collaboration of all stakeholders. Linking the power of collaborative leadership with the promise of public engagement produces a strong momentum toward the achievement of organizational excellence. Naturally linked by common principles, engagement of and collaboration among the stakeholders produces the culture required for individuals to contribute their wisdom to finding solutions for the organizational problems of today. Collaborative leadership requires the engagement of all stakeholders, and this engagement is the subject of the next chapter.

5

*Engage the Public
in a Productive and
Proactive Manner*

> *The presence of emotion in public life is essential if people are to
> form and sustain relationships with public concerns.*
>
> —Richard Harwood (1993)

NINE FACTORS OF ENGAGEMENT

Some of the answers to the challenge of meaningful public engagement can be found in a publication entitled *Meaningful Chaos: How People Form Relationships With Public Concerns*, a report prepared for the Kettering Foundation by the Harwood Group of Bethesda, Maryland, and published in 1993. This report concludes that there are nine factors important to the manner in which citizens form and maintain relationships with public concerns (1993, p. 1). It follows that knowledge of these factors incorporated into policy considerations regarding the involvement of the public in decision making will enrich and improve decisions and relationships between schools and their publics. These nine factors are summarized as follows: *

- Connections—People tend to enlarge, rather than narrow, their views of public concerns, making connections among ideas and topics that society tends to fragment.

- Personal Context—People relate to concerns that "fit" with their personal context—not only their own self-interest, but that which is meaningful or imaginable to them in their lives.

- Coherence—People want public discourse to tell the 'whole story' on public concerns—with explanation, memory, and a sense of overview. They are seeking a deeper sense of understanding and meaning.

- Room for Ambivalence—People resist polarization on public concerns, seeking instead room for ambivalence—a gray area in the public debate in which to question, discuss, test ideas, and gain confidence about their views.

- Emotion—The presence of emotion in public life is essential if people are to form and sustain relationships with public concerns.

- Authenticity—Information and individuals must 'ring true' to people—reflecting to people a basic sense of reality and the general belief that they are being squared with.

- Sense of Possibilities—People are seeking a sense of possibility—that action might occur on a public concern, and that they might play a personal role in it.

- Catalysts—Everyday Americans, not just experts and elites, are key catalysts in helping people form relationships with public concerns.

- Mediating Institutions—Mediating institutions are places where people come together to talk and act on public concerns. (1993, pp. 7-37)

*Reprinted with permission from The Kettering Foundation.

PUBLIC INVOLVEMENT

When we consider the substance of these Nine Factors, we discover that we cannot incorporate these factors into our traditional notion of how organizations operate. To do so is certainly tantamount to upsetting the traditional hierarchy of schools. We cannot hold the notions of traditional management principles near and dear and at the same time profit from the virtues of public engagement.

Traditional administrative practice often causes more controversy by refusing to engage in discussion regarding issues perceived to be controversial. Using these Nine Factors to influence our decisions regarding public involvement meaningfully changes how schools relate to their publics (see Figure 5.1). From the Kettering work, we now know that public organizations can garnish support by demonstrating a willingness to engage the public.

BUILDING PRINCIPALS AND THE NINE FACTORS

What does engaging the public look like at the school building level? What changes in how the building principal leads others are necessary in order to capitalize on what the Nine Factors teach us? The following represents suggestions for building principals to take full advantage of what we have learned from the Nine Factors:

1. Connections—Replace *reporting to* the stakeholders with *thinking with* them. This requires meaningful discussions with teachers and parents instead of reading aloud the minutes from the last meeting. The principal must establish a dialogue in which everybody feels comfortable enough to participate. He or she must explain the facts underlying the whole story, the whole problem, or the whole challenge.

Often building principals make the mistake of assuming that because a problem seems unsolvable to them, it will seem unsolvable to all. This assumption precludes the power of engaging the public and the combined wisdom that will reveal itself with meaningful discussion among the school stakeholders.

Building principals should facilitate the discussion to sharply focus on the problem or challenge. For the purpose of solving complex school problems, the principal should consider weekly meetings in which he or she shares the relationships between the various components of the problem and facilitates dialogue with the stakeholders about these components and their relationships. Again, this practice will open the door for the combined wisdom of the group to suggest solutions to the problem. The relationships between school curriculum and the instructional program, athletics and the school vision, and feedback from parents and the consequent changes in the various components of an educational program surveyed, all serve as examples of important relationships in need of common understanding among the stakeholders.

2. Personal Context—Stakeholders engaged in meaningful decision making need to be able to envision what the problem or challenge will look like when it is solved. When dealing with parents regarding their children, it is not difficult to help them see their personal stake in the educational problem or challenge. The building principal should facilitate discussions based upon common experiences of the stakeholders where appropriate. For example, focusing upon experiences with children at

Figure 5.1   Public Involvement

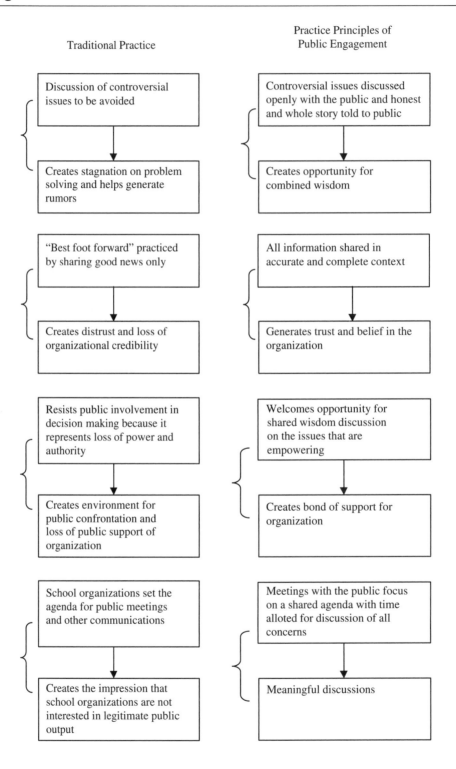

school that are similar to experiences with children at home frames the discussion in a personal context. Whenever possible, discussions with parents should be based upon common experiences with children at home and at school. Attention problems at home can be discussed in relation to attention problems at school. Engaging stakeholders in school concerns should be facilitated in such a manner as to make it possible for the stakeholder to see common elements from their own personal context in those of other stakeholders. In this way, individual stakeholders become more effectively engaged.

3. Coherence—For a number of reasons, including credibility that generates trust, it is incumbent upon the building principal to always tell the whole story regarding a school concern. As the building principal shares and explains the whole story, he or she should add to the coherence of the story by making helpful links to ideas commonly understood by all. In addition, most "whole story" explanations often lend themselves well to experiences the stakeholders already have in common from past school discussions and problem-solving conversations.

4. Room for Ambivalence—If we are to capitalize upon what we have learned about public engagement, building principals must learn that ambivalence on issues will not be resolved by individual stakeholders in isolation from one another. In this sense, working through ambivalence is a group activity. Stakeholders must be given the opportunity for conversations reflecting differences of opinion and various points of view, especially about gray and uncertain issues.

Ultimately, shared decision making by a group of stakeholders will reduce or eliminate ambivalence otherwise found to be prevalent. Schools today need increased opportunities for parents, teachers, and community members to ask questions and learn from one another regarding complex public school issues.

5. Emotion—Making decisions is not exclusively an intellectual process. Many principals have been trained to refrain from revealing their feelings when working professionally. While this is certainly good advice for those everyday applications of rules and regulations within schools, it is not helpful for the productive involvement of stakeholders in shared decision making regarding the more conceptually challenging issues facing schools today. Principals must set the example by honestly sharing their feelings along with the facts and opinions related to the issues under discussion. The objective here is not to sway opinion by so doing, but rather to simply encourage others to do the same and thereby set a tone of amicable discourse about disagreement on the component issues of a problem. Solutions are developed more effectively and productively with the transformation of amicable disagreement into combined group wisdom.

6.   Authenticity—Principals need to be candid and sometimes frank about the issues involved with shared decision making. Stakeholders will judge information or the individual presenting the information to be authentic when they are convinced that the information as well as the individual presenting the information are consistent with their own experiences. Principals must be aware of experiences stakeholders have had in the past regarding school issues and problems. In order to avoid unresolved problems from the past interfering with productive shared decision making in the future, he or she must address them frankly and honestly. When the group discussion leads to conclusions which seem to be inconsistent with the experiences of the group, the principal must engage the group in a learning process in order to produce new understandings that are more consistent with group conclusions. One manner of accomplishing this is simply to facilitate group discussion of "new" knowledge. In these discussions, new understandings of concepts important to effective group decision making can be achieved. For example, group study and discussion of the notion of "connections" from the Kettering study of the Nine Factors of public engagement would sharpen the focus of each stakeholder on the importance of developing unifying threads in their decision making, while at the same time avoiding fragmentation of issues. In this manner, mistaken notions and misunderstandings can be replaced with clear and informed insights helpful to the task of creating improved opportunities for student learning. In this fashion, both the principal and the process are validated as authentic. Without this learning process, change is difficult. The possibility for action on the deliberations of the stakeholders is also important for the process to be viewed as authentic. In order for the principal to be accepted as authentic by the stakeholders, he or she must have a track record of putting into action shared decisions made in the past.

7.   Sense of Possibilities—Stakeholders must feel through their experiences that what they have to say will have an impact on the shared decision, and that the decision will make a difference in schools. The principal is in the position to facilitate the discussions so that everyone involved can participate in a meaningful process, and that they understand the different opinions and views of the group. The principal must exemplify the degree of patience and understanding necessary for seemingly conflicting views or interpretations to finally come together into a truly combined, group wisdom. When this happens, the sense of possibilities is underscored in a very positive way.

8.   Catalysts—Catalysts, in this context, are people relied upon by others to help them make decisions about public issues. These catalysts are respected and believable. In order for a building principal to serve as a catalyst for school stakeholders he or she must exhibit a close congruence

between what he or she says and does. Moreover, he or she must relate to stakeholders in a caring way. Principals must be perceived as sincerely and personally invested in the shared decision making of the stakeholders. The principal must be able to guide the group of decision makers based upon their respect for his or her honesty. How they are viewed in this category of the Nine Factors is closely related to other factors such as authenticity.

9. Mediating Institutions—Principals must form authentic partnerships with leaders of local organizations such as churches, local government, local industry, and service organizations. It is in these settings that community members gather and discuss important issues. Principals should initiate and maintain open communications with those who hold ongoing conversations with community members. Designation of a "Key Communicators" group with whom the principal meets on a regular basis helps these catalysts to stir interest in schools and explain current school issues. By so doing, the principal gains more informed decision makers with whom he or she can work to improve schools.

DEEPER PUBLIC INVOLVEMENT

The involvement of the public in public schools is a two-way street. There is much to gain from a deeper involvement of the public in their schools and the schools in their public. Forging stronger partnerships between school and home can only improve performance of students at school and quality of life in the home. Lisbeth B. Schorr, in her book, *Common Purpose,* underscores this importance:

> Schools increasingly recognize the need for deeper parent involvement. They are aware that enlisting the overwhelmed and overstressed parents of today as collaborators requires more skill and ingenuity than ever before. In many communities the new partnership transforms schools into community centers. In others, schools join forces with community institutions to help strengthen families—be it through family support services, the child welfare system, or churches. Successful programs then, do not substitute for strong families, but they have the ability to support families' capacities to raise strong families. (1997, p. 7)

In order to take a snapshot in time of where a school or district is on the scale of public engagement, the following survey is offered:

Figure 5.2 Public Engagement Survey

On a scale of 1-5 with 5 being the highest, assign a number to best represent your school/district rating on each item.

	1	2	3	4	5
Our school/district regularly meets with parents and the public, using an agenda developed in partnership with the public.	☐	☐	☐	☐	☐
Our school/district regularly seeks written feedback from parents that assesses their perception of "being meaningfully involved."	☐	☐	☐	☐	☐
Our parents and public are meaningfully involved in conversations with us regarding the future.	☐	☐	☐	☐	☐
Professional staff members at our school/district sincerely believe the public can help us do our job better.	☐	☐	☐	☐	☐
We have a systematic and regularly implemented process of involving parents in decision making about our curriculum.	☐	☐	☐	☐	☐
Our school district has a current strategic plan, the development of which involved a wide cross section of our community.	☐	☐	☐	☐	☐
Our school/district schedules time for educators and community members to exchange ideas about school/district progress.	☐	☐	☐	☐	☐
Our parents believe that action will occur on legitimate issues they bring to our school/district.	☐	☐	☐	☐	☐
Our parents feel that they will be called upon to help make school decisions.	☐	☐	☐	☐	☐
Our school/district has formed a positive working relationship with parents.	☐	☐	☐	☐	☐

S.W.A.T. TEAMS: SCHOOLS WHERE ACHIEVEMENT THRIVES

Developing within the stakeholders the skills of the Five Essentials produces the environment in Schools Where Achievement Thrives (SWAT). Students achieving at maximum potential is a reflection of the effectiveness of the stakeholders. There is a momentum and a rhythm that develops, generating a productive and successful culture within such schools. Morale and a sense of belonging soar. Teachers, administrators, parents, and board members are able to achieve their personal goals while utilizing their five essential skills to accomplish the district mission. Knowing they are an important part of a high-performance team only motivates them to become more significantly involved. Exemplary performance is very self-rewarding. The performance of such schools then becomes the bench-marking standard against which others measure themselves.

KITCHEN TALKS

When, as a superintendent, I found parents reluctant to come to school to discuss issues, parents who were disenchanted with past experiences with their schools, I developed "Kitchen Talk." I visited the homes of these parents and held informal discussions that proved to be an excellent way in which to engage them successfully. We sat down around the kitchen table, broke bread, and engaged in discussions related to student learning issues *as the parents viewed them.* I immediately noticed the passion and emotion threaded throughout all they had to say. We know from the Kettering research found in their publication *Meaningful Chaos* that one of the Nine Factors of public engagement is the presence of emotion.

Soon I realized that their vision of what was best for *their children* was the same vision I had for *our students.* We agreed on the "what" but not on the "how." What differed was how we achieved the vision. These parents related feelings of disenfranchisement, which created a different set of obstacles than I had envisioned. I confessed that what they were telling me was a revelation to me, and I anticipated that they would chastise me for not knowing their true feelings, but their response pleasantly surprised me. They explained that simply because I had taken the initiative to listen to them, they viewed me as the champion of the possibility for their children to receive a quality education. Their need for meaningful dialogue and understanding of their problems was so great that the smallest indication of the school to enter into the discussion created mountains of hope they had not felt before. The issues were not easy, but there was a natural civility and flow to the conversations. This engagement, when coupled with the other essential elements of the transformation of schools, produced dramatic improvements in student achievement in just one academic year.

SCHOOL BLOCK TALK

School Block Talk was developed as a result of a superintendent's experience in a school district of approximately 30,000 students. In his first year as superintendent, he determined that the best way to learn the needs of students throughout the district was to visit each school and meet with teachers, administrators, and parents of students attending the school. The district was predominantly white on the west side of the district and black on the east side. A heavy concentration of disadvantaged families was located on the east side. When he visited the west side schools, a typical turnout of parents, teachers, and administrators totaled over 100 people, equally represented by teachers, administrators, and parents. The conversation was productive and very helpful and informative for him.

This was not the case when he visited east side schools. In his first several east side school visits, only two or three parents were in attendance. When he questioned the parents who were at the gathering regarding the absence of other parents, their response was both surprising and understandable. They commented that these minority parents generally encountered negative experiences when they visited their child's school. They were invited to school only when there was an academic or discipline problem with their child. Consequently, it was not a positive experience for them. They were therefore unable to benefit from any proactive conversation and suggestions for improving their student's opportunities for learning. When the superintendent asked why the father relating this explanation was there, he replied that he had served 15 years in prison for drug dealing and was now determined, against all odds, to create a better environment for his child because his child's education was extremely important to him. His story was powerful and compelling.

School Block Talk was designed as a means to reach minority parents reluctant to come to school. The concept was simple: Respect their reasons for not coming to school and take the school to them. Arrangements were made for the superintendent to meet with east side parents on their own turf, at churches and community meeting rooms in their own neighborhoods.

The results were astonishing. At the first meeting, 150 parents showed up and had productive conversation with the superintendent from seven in the evening until midnight. Everyone present knew that the meeting was judged to be a success by the parents when they were asked, "What last question do you have for the superintendent?" The parents' response was, "When is the superintendent coming back?"

School Block Talk was designed to incorporate what had been learned about the needs of parents on the east side of the school district. Informal two-way communication combined with celebrations of learning potential for students were scheduled at each of the east-side schools. These celebrations were held on Saturdays throughout the school year.

Experience teaches us to believe in quality conversation and sympathetic listening. Conversation regarding the learning needs of the parents' children and the school district's students was the common bond of School Block Talk. The School Block Talk events were scheduled as all-day affairs. While the traditional groups of the school community, school board members, parents, teachers, and administrators were invited, the event planners were happily surprised by the turnout of much more of the community. Ministers, church congregation members, local disk jockeys, community political leaders, university faculty members, realtors, and many others from the community turned out for these events, which quickly became local "happenings."

There was music, food reflective of the community culture, entertainment from local talent, and recognition of student achievement. These events became ongoing rallies in support of student achievement. They were so effective and so well received that west side schools soon emulated them.

PRINCIPAL-LED PARENTAL COLLABORATION

Principal-led parental collaboration is presented here as a guide for the local development of programs tailored to meet individual school needs. Such programs can be implemented easily in order to provide meaningful involvement of parents and other community adults in the academic achievement of students. These guidelines are designed to provide a sense of stability, support, and security to students while developing a solid working relationship between school, home, and community. The goal is improved academic achievement. Using collaborative leadership skills, the building principal should utilize the following guidelines to facilitate the accomplishment of this goal:

• Academic Cross-Functional Support Team—Made up of cross-sectional representation from parents and other community members, this collaborative team is trained in collaboration skills. Members from this team provide remedial tutoring, classroom teacher assistance, and two-way communication between home and school for each classroom in the building. Wherever possible, partnerships are formed with employers to secure release of collaborative team members for school service.

• School/Community Meetings—Throughout the course of the academic school year, weekend meetings are scheduled for each classroom. During this time, academic and social activities are scheduled. Facilitated by individual members of the Academic Cross-Functional Support Team, academic progress, academic counseling, and individual learning strategies for each student are updated by parents and teachers. At each meeting, individual student successes are recognized and celebrated.

• Parent Workshops—Relationships between home and school are developed, targeting a shared responsibility for student achievement. Prior to the start of the school year, the first of a weekly series of parent workshops is scheduled. Conducted by classroom teachers, these weekly workshops are scheduled at a time convenient to parents and are geared to provide knowledge and understanding of both their child's curriculum and the skills parents need to support and direct, at home, their child's classroom instruction. Parental knowledge of specific curricula is scheduled to precede their child's study of that same curriculum experience. The time parents spend in these workshops will enable them to spend unlimited productive hours with their children at home. Parents also become members of the local Leadership Academy for the purpose of developing skills to collaborate with the school to increase their child's achievement.

• Collaborative Teaching-Learning Teams—Teachers are assigned to Collaborative Teaching-Learning Teams designed to focus on individual student rates of development and learning styles. In addition to his or her classroom teacher, each student is assigned to a member of a Collaborative Teaching-Learning Team. In this manner, individual student achievement is tracked and monitored and, based on these results, appropriate modifications in individual student learning experiences are made on a continuous basis. Parents are continuously updated regarding these modifications.

• Focus on Results—Student achievement measures as well as student attendance rates, student disciplinary referrals, and staff attendance are monitored and reported to all on a regular basis. The Academic Cross-Functional Support Team studies these results and makes recommendations regarding strategies for improvement of these measures when necessary. In addition, parent concerns regarding these measures are addressed.

Principal-led parental collaboration can be locally adapted and represents effective guidelines for parental involvement in student achievement. In response to school district, building, and teacher accountability to the state's standardized testing programs, these guidelines involve parents directly in the instructional process for increased student achievement. Through frequent meetings on teaching objectives in core subjects, constant communication between home and school, and celebration of student successes, principal-led parental collaboration emphasizes the attainment of academic excellence across all subjects.

In their book entitled *Ten Steps to a Learning Organization*, Peter Kline and Bernard Saunders point out that "we're almost totally unaccustomed to the spontaneous discovery of each other's talents and skills. But it is these vast and varied capabilities of its workforce (not the range of their job descriptions) which make up the greatest resource of an organization" (1993, p. 110). Educators must learn and accept new ways of profiting from the wisdom and talents of the people around them. But to do so requires that we let go of the artifacts from our past. This has proven to be a difficult task. We tend to strongly "habitualize" routine and organizational processes that we view as crucial to our successes of the past.

In public education today, we find little support for risk taking. This, of course, precludes dramatically the opportunity for educators to learn from failure. Little failures along the way teach us—they steer us on the road to success. It has been said that mistakes are errors that go uncorrected. In an environment unsupportive of risk taking, little can be learned from errors never experienced. Mistakes made in an honest effort to improve learning opportunities for students are an acceptable part of the process of improving public education today. Fear of failure should not be permitted to serve as a deterrent to improvement.

Principals must receive support from the school board to initiate new and modify old educational programs in an effort to improve instruction and curriculum. In too many instances, this is not the case. Again, meaningful conversations characterized by frank, yet supportive, and candid, yet helpful, dialogue among school leaders creates the comfort level for risk taking that offers better learning opportunities for our students.

SUMMARY

Since the report from the Harwood Group, *Meaningful Chaos: How People Form Relationships With Public Concerns,* we now know the factors important to the manner in which citizens form and maintain relationships with public concerns. Using these factors as part of the equation to transform public schools improves the quality of involvement and the subsequent decision making. Because of the nature of these factors, they do not lend themselves to our traditional school organizational forms. We need to replace the tensions caused by the traditional practice of a "we, they" approach to leadership of our schools with the productive engagement of parents and other stakeholders that reflects a "we together" attitude of collaborative school leadership. We cannot sustain traditional organizational forms and at the same time profit from the virtues of public engagement.

The talents and capabilities of the stakeholders of public education today represent both the greatest resource and the most underutilized area of public school organizations. When we compare traditional practice with the principles of public engagement, we discover major differences. With the public productively engaged in the decision making within our public schools, we can deal constructively with controversial issues, share our wisdom, generate trust and belief in the organization, create a bond of support for the organization, and develop ongoing meaningful discussions.

More programs similar to School Block Talk, Kitchen Talks, and Principal-Led Parental Collaboration are needed in order to fully maximize the learning opportunities for students based on shared understanding of the challenges facing the home as well as the school.

It is vital that the public be given every opportunity to become engaged in the process of collaborative decision making regarding the Five Essentials. Because the standards of excellence set the mark for high performance within a school district, nowhere is it more important that the public be authentically involved than in the process of developing these standards. Governance by standards is the subject of our next chapter.

6

Govern by Standards Developed With the Stakeholders

Public education in America is, in the most fundamental sense, a public issue. Schools will not change because leaders want them to. They will change when parents, students, and teachers go about their daily activities in different ways. That will only happen when the public is considered an equal and respected partner in reform—one whose views are worth listening to.

—Deborah Wadsworth (from Johnson & Immerwahr, 1994)

BUILDING PRINCIPALS AND THE NEED FOR STANDARDS OF EXCELLENCE

First, in order to develop a learning organization capable of high performance, it is necessary to understand completely the formal and informal decision-making patterns currently in place. Boards of governance often make decisions in a reactive mode. Accordingly, there develops a lack of consistency or alignment to an overall mission from one decision to the next. Of course, this leads to the appearance of favoritism and bias toward those in the school community with interests in particular issues. Every governance board has been faced with the embarrassment of trying to justify decisions the basis of which has no alignment to any given set of criteria.

At the individual school level, in the absence of standards of excellence, building principals must make decisions affecting the quality of their educational program without the benefit of guidance from uniform and consistent performance criteria. Without standards of excellence serving as a point of reference, decisions such as teacher assignments, curriculum revisions, teacher evaluations, and parental involvement can easily appear to be unfair and reflective of favoritism.

In addition, since these standards of excellence are developed with the active engagement and representation from all the stakeholders, they embody the combined wisdom of those who will be affected by decisions based on them. Thus, the building principal is legitimately empowered to facilitate the application of these standards on a daily basis as opposed to making decisions solely on the power of his or her authority of position. In addition, student needs relative to the standards can more effectively be matched to the specific expertise of individual teachers, and curriculum adjustments can be more legitimately justified to parents and teachers alike.

The strategic plan of the school district sets the stage for the development of standards. The mission statement, strategies, and action plans define the parameters and expectations of the standards. The standards should be aligned with the strategic plan. In this manner, they become standards of excellence, reflecting the purpose, function, and expectations of excellence within each area of service in the school district. It is important to note that neither the standards alone nor the strategic plan alone can accomplish this.

DEVELOPING STANDARDS OF EXCELLENCE CONSISTENT WITH SCHOOL VISION

Like the mission of the school district, the vision of the school should reflect both intention and purpose. Changes in how the school operates begin with an analysis of what is required to achieve the school vision. The following represents guidelines for determining standards of excellence that align with the strategic plan and contribute to the ultimate accomplishment of the school vision:

    A. Using conjoined conversation techniques (p. 3) and deciding by consensus, a cross-functional team of parents, teachers, and administrators should determine the implications and requirements for each of the school service areas underlying the school vision.

Figure 6.1 Service Areas and Standards Compliance

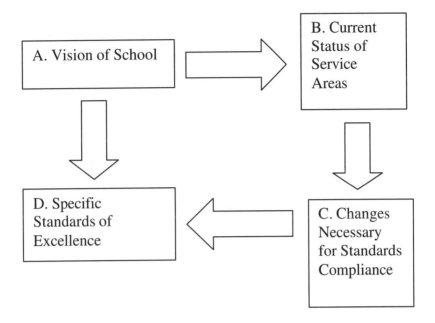

B. Determine the current status of each service area relative to the requirements derived in A above.

C. Determine the changes necessary in each service area to meet the requirements of A above.

What often is missing in efforts to accomplish a school vision is consistency between what is agreed upon as the school vision and what is done operationally to accomplish it. Figure 6.1 demonstrates the conceptual relationship between the vision of the school, standards of excellence, and the current status of the various service areas relative to both the vision and the standards. Standards of excellence that are subsequently developed should be inspired by and compatible with the school vision.

For individual schools operating within a school district with a well-developed strategic plan, there should also be a high degree of consistency among the school vision, school standards of excellence, and the school district mission. While a strategic plan for a school district should set parameters for individual schools through its articulated mission and strategies, indicators of how the district will accomplish the mission, if we are to capitalize upon the creative energies and combined wisdom of the stakeholders, the parameters set by the district plan should be wide and broadly stated in order for individual schools to focus upon their unique set of circumstances and develop their vision and standards accordingly.

For the purpose of developing and recognizing high-performing schools, standards of excellence should meet the following criteria:

- Standards of excellence should be established by representational stakeholder consent.
- Standards of excellence should reflect the minimum acceptable standards to qualify for the recognition of excellence in performance by all stakeholders, especially students.
- Standards of excellence should have highly recognized, widely accepted, and permanent educational value.

Certainly the development of standards of excellence should engage those affected by the standards themselves. The spirit, philosophy, and underlying purpose that make a school or school district unique will be the same in both the strategic plan and the standards of excellence. Those who help develop the strategic plan can contribute much to the development of the standards of excellence.

Schools and school districts are expected to be accountable for the level of student achievement. The combination of the strategic plan and the standards of excellence enables the school or school district to be accountable at all times.

GOVERN BY STANDARDS

Appropriately, school boards are expected to be accountable for the level of student achievement throughout the school district. But accountable as defined by what standard and accountable to standards determined by what process and involving what groups of people? Movement across the states has produced de facto curriculum imposition on school districts by way of statewide proficiency testing. Does this represent grass roots control or should it? Whatever your answers are to these questions, we cannot achieve excellence in learning without defining the standard of excellence. Excellence should define the standard whether emanating from the national, state, or local level. Excellence defines the standard. Only if we have standards of excellence can we measure our progress toward meeting them. Where we find we are not incompliance with a standard, then a quality assurance program should outline restoration of compliance with that standard. Standards should be drafted within a school district for the following general basic program service areas:

1. School Board
   1.1 Membership on the School Board
   1.2 Functions of the School Board
   1.3 Relationship of the School Board and Administration
   1.4 School Board Policy

2. Human Resources and Instructional Services
   2.1 Staff Development and Evaluation

        2.2 Instructional Services
        2.3 Problem Solving Development
        2.4 Instructional Evaluation
        2.5 Participatory Management Development
        2.6 Recruitment and Selection

    3. Curricular and Pupil Personnel Services
        3.1 Curriculum Plan
        3.2 Curriculum Management System
        3.3 Curriculum Selection Criteria
        3.4 Curriculum Structuring Criteria
        3.5 Co Curricular Programs

    4. Educational Program Design and Special Education Services
        4.1 Student Services
        4.2 Special Services, Census, Home Instruction
        4.3 Overall Curriculum Evaluation
        4.4 Ongoing Strategic Planning
        4.5 Quality Assurance Program
        4.6 Research

Clearly, in order to govern by standards developed by the stakeholders, we must have the commitment and support of the school board as well as the other stakeholders. The following two standards represent examples that apply to the governing body:

Standard 1.2. Functions of the Board of Education

The board of education functions primarily as a policy-making body, strives to carry out its function in accordance with the district's mission statement, and serves the needs of the student population.

It is important that the board of education demonstrates its commitment to the meaningful involvement of all stakeholders in the school or school district. By including this reference to the mission statement from the school district strategic plan, the school board underscores its commitment to operate in accordance with both the meaningful involvement of the stakeholders and the decisions these stakeholders make.

In order for this governance program to function effectively, there must be a recognition of and adherence to well-defined roles and responsibilities by all involved, especially the governing board. In the following governance standard of excellence, the school board stresses the importance of understanding the difference between the role of the school board and that of the administration:

Standard 1.3. Relationship of the Board of Education to Administration

Roles and functional services of both the board of education and administration are clearly understood by all those involved. Job performance responsibilities of all administrators are commonly understood by the board of education and administration alike.

All too often, confusion about roles and responsibilities of the school board versus the administration produces counterproductive efforts and a lack of trust and understanding that undermines the achievement of excellence in education these standards are designed to accomplish. Including a standard which specifies a commitment to clearly defined responsibilities sends a strong signal to building principals and other stakeholders that there is and will be support for their efforts to transform their school in order to meet the standards of excellence "trusted" by all stakeholders.

The following examples represent building-level standards compatible with the district-level standard:

Standard 2.1. Staff Development and Evaluation—District Standard

The board of education promotes excellence in teaching through the integration of the process of evaluation and staff development. Such a program offers the opportunity for each teacher to develop his or her potential as an instructor.

Standard 2.1.1 Teacher Evaluation and Development—Building Standard

The evaluation of teachers incorporates both self-evaluation and administrator appraisal. Each teacher appraisal will incorporate feedback from peers and a professional development plan.

Emphasis in Standard 2.1.1 on self-evaluation and the incorporation of a professional development plan underscores the worth of those being evaluated by communicating the importance of the engagement of staff members in the process of evaluation as well as school decision making in general. But the standard does not speak only to evaluation. In keeping with the district standard, the building-level standard addresses a proactive inclusion of a staff development plan as well as feedback from peers. In this manner, honest dialogue regarding plans targeted to improve teaching, and thereby learning, can be conducted in a trusting and supportive fashion.

Standard 2.2. Instructional Services—District Standard

The board of education recognizes the importance of a sound educational program in meeting the requirements of the district's mission statement. The selection of content for instructional services is determined jointly by faculty and administration and is individualized to meet the needs and interests of the students.

Standard 2.2.1 Instructional Services—Building Standard

Cross-functional teams of parents, teachers, and administrators will review and select curriculum based on student achievement results on standardized tests and the district mission statement.

The building-level standard in this example specifies the use of standardized student achievement test results and the district mission statement as the points of reference in determining curriculum selection. In addition, the building-level standard requires representation from all school site stakeholders as the team empowered to select curriculum in accordance with specified selection criteria.

Standard 2.4. Instructional Evaluation—District Standard

The school district utilizes a systematic evaluation of both the effectiveness and appropriateness of the instructional program. Such a program review provides for the continuous review of educational goals stressing the interrelation of the curricula.

Standard 2.4.1 Instructional Evaluation—Building Standard

The instructional program will be evaluated on an annual basis by a cross-functional team of parents, administrators, and teachers. Student achievement results will be compared to instructional objectives, educational goals, and the design of the integrated curriculum. A survey of teachers and parents will be used to determine the appropriateness of the instructional objectives.

The building-level standard in this instance commits the school site to the requirements of the district-level standard. In addition, it defines membership on the evaluation team. It also specifies that this evaluation team, utilizing an "appropriateness survey" administered to teachers and parents, will determine the appropriateness of the instructional objectives. This building-level standard also reflects that this school site has implemented an integrated curriculum program.

Standard 3.1. Plan of the Curriculum—District Standard

The curricula are based on educational goals that reflect the district's mission statement. There is a direct and obvious relationship between these goals and the components of the curricula.

Standard 3.1.1 Plan of the Curriculum—Building Standard

A cross-functional team of teachers, administrators, and parents will construct instructional objectives derived directly from the district mission statement and the district educational goals. Once these instructional objectives are developed, this cross-functional team will develop specific learning objectives to be compatible with the educational goals and instructional objectives.

This building-level standard clearly sets forth how the learning objectives of this school site will be determined. It ties the process directly back to the district mission statement in the district-level standard.

Standard 4.5. Ongoing Strategic Planning—District Standard

The school board promotes an ongoing program of strategic planning, drawing from a broad base of participation involving both staff and community members.

Standard 4.5.1 Ongoing Strategic Planning—Building Standard

A strategic planning team composed of parents, teachers, and administrators will review the strategic plan of the school on a semi-annual basis. Prior to the start of the school year, this team will make recommendations for modifications of the school strategic plan to the building principal. This team will evaluate compliance with school-level and district-level standards as the determining factor in making these recommendations.

The district standard in this example is drafted in a broad fashion. This allows the building standard to be determined from a larger set of options.

Many individual buildings operating within school districts today do so in the absence of any recognizable curricular/instructional connection to the school district to which they belong. In some cases, they operate very independently. There are many reasons for this, but in too many cases, building principals are forced to operate independently because of out-of-date school board policies that are unresponsive to student needs and are in serious need of revision. Many principals of these schools, in order to meet student needs, either find exceptions to these rules or simply ignore them.

One of the primary strengths of governance by standards is that this system allows individual buildings rather wide latitude in each service area. In this fashion, individual building needs and circumstances, including student need differences between buildings, within a school district can be appropriately addressed. This allows the school sites to better reach their potential in terms of standards of excellence.

THE GOVERNANCE MODEL

This model focuses on the operational delivery of public school district services. District services are divided into the following categories:

Community Communication and Information Services

Human Resources

Instructional Services

Curricular and Pupil Personnel Services

The evaluation of the delivery of services in each of these areas incorporates four general components:

1. Development of Standards of Excellence

As previously discussed, the school community should be involved in the development of these standards. Individuals should participate on the basis of expertise and or interest. These standards represent the minimum standard of acceptability that each service area is expected to achieve.

2. Completion of Self-Study of Service Areas

Led by the service area director, evaluation teams composed of stakeholders from both the staff and community complete a self-study of the department's delivery of services. Each department is evaluated against standards of excellence for that particular area.

3. Review of the Service Area by the Compliance Review Team

A team of experts from outside the school district reviews each service area self-study. After reviewing the self-studies, the compliance review team evaluates the service area against the appropriate standards of excellence and reports its findings to the board of governance.

4. Quality Restoration Team

If deficiencies are noted by the compliance review team, a quality restoration team is convened to review the report and prepare actions/ solutions for restoration of any area of non-compliance along with a time line for its achievement.

Whereas standards represent the minimum requirement, each service area is expected to meet the standards at the level judged acceptable by the compliance review team at the time of its evaluation. However, each service area is expected to continue to raise its expectations as time passes so as to be constantly improving. Thus, each new evaluation will raise the standards.

Evaluation of each service area against standards specifically written for that service area fulfills three functions:

Figure 6.2 Standards of Excellence Survey

For each question, indicate which answer describes your perception of your job situation, Strongly Agree (SA), Agree (A), Disagree (D), or Strongly Disagree (SD).

	SA	A	D	SD
1. In my school/district, standards defining excellence are clearly written and communicated.	☐	☐	☐	☐
2. In my school/district, we evaluate ourselves against these standards of excellence on a regular basis.	☐	☐	☐	☐
3. As part of our department/school/division meetings, we target and measure continuous progress toward meeting the school/district standards of excellence.	☐	☐	☐	☐
4. We use student results data to measure our progress toward meeting academic standards of excellence.	☐	☐	☐	☐
5. Most people feel the standards of excellence in our school/district are reflective of top performance.	☐	☐	☐	☐
6. As an educator in my school/district, I am supplied with data analysis important to my role in improving learning opportunities for students.	☐	☐	☐	☐
7. Our school/district measures its progress toward meeting these standards of excellence at least quarterly.	☐	☐	☐	☐
8. The standards of excellence for my school/district help me better understand my job responsibilities.	☐	☐	☐	☐
9. In my school/district, there is alignment between our standards of excellence and the allocation of resources.	☐	☐	☐	☐
10. In my school/district, the standards of excellence reflect ambitious yet realistic comprehensive goals.	☐	☐	☐	☐

1. Evaluation assures that each service area offers quality delivery of services that focus ultimately on learner outcomes.

2. Evaluation ensures restoration of quality services where needed.

3. Evaluation advances the purpose of education through improvement of services offered.

As a result of the implementation of the governance model, school districts profit from a continuous and reliable system of improvement in the services it provides. Ultimately, it is the utilization of this program that drives the improvement of student learning.

Figure 6.2 presents a survey that will begin to orient the staff to the operational implementation of standards of excellence.

SUMMARY

Much has been debated and written about standards defining excellence in American schools. Should we adopt national educational standards? Should we continue with the trend of student proficiency testing based upon statewide educational standards currently in place in many states? Regardless of the answers to these questions, local school districts can and should set their own standards of excellence consistent with their unique mission. The strategic plan of a school organization sets the tone for the development of these standards of excellence. This development utilizes the skills of leading collaboratively, benchmarking for excellence, planning strategically, and engaging the public.

The governance model presented in this chapter outlines a quality assurance program that is aligned with the standards of excellence as well as the mission statement of the organization. Governance boils down to decision making. Ultimately, governing boards are responsible for the decisions made, but shared decision-making produces more effective educational results. More effective educational results produce more effective learning. Governing by standards enhances the educational stakeholders' abilities and proclivities to engage in shared decision making.

Establishing standards of excellence creates the opportunity for organizations to continuously monitor their progress toward the goal of achieving organizational excellence, which is precisely what is required by the the Baldrige Quality System and the Sterling Criteria for Organizational Performance Excellence. Many of the criteria included in these systems incorporate the principles of the Five Essentials for the transformation of schools. In Chapter 7, I discuss how the Five Essentials empower integrated management systems.

7

Empower Integrated Management Systems With Five Essential Skills

The interior and exterior selves are best integrated within a setting in which the individual and the collective are also brought together. This enables people to change as they buy into larger organizational changes in a genuine fusion of mutual interests.

—Richard L. Daft and Robert H. Lengel (1998)

THE STERLING CRITERIA FOR ORGANIZATIONAL PERFORMANCE EXCELLENCE

The Florida Sterling Council was established by executive order of the Governor of Florida. It is a public/private partnership. The Florida Sterling Criteria for Organizational Performance Excellence are based on the Malcolm Baldrige Quality Award Criteria. In their publication, *The 2000 Sterling Criteria for Organizational Performance Excellence*, The Florida Sterling Council stipulates that,

> The Sterling Criteria for Organizational Performance Excellence are designed to assist organizations to continually improve how they do business. The criteria are based on an integrated set of basic values, requirements, and processes aimed at increasing customer value and driving organizational effectiveness. It is a self-assessment tool to help organizations determine their current capabilities, including their strengths and areas where improvement is needed.
>
> The Governors Sterling Award is based on the Sterling Criteria for Organizational Performance Excellence and is specifically designed to promote, encourage, and recognize excellence based on the principles of leadership, employee involvement, customer satisfaction, and continuous improvement. (Florida Sterling Council, 2000, p. iv)

The skills of the Five Essentials can be productively applied to this system of integrated management and this application lends itself effectively to public school systems. In the same publication, The Sterling Council presents the following criteria for excellence (2000, p. 1). The core values and concepts are embodied in seven categories as follows:

1. Leadership
2. Strategic Planning
3. Customer and Market Focus
4. Information and Analysis
5. Human Resource Focus
6. Process Management
7. Business Results

Reprinted with permission from The Florida Sterling Council.

PRINCIPALS, FIVE ESSENTIALS, AND STERLING

The Sterling Criteria are broken into more specific areas and pose questions of the organization in order to determine whether or not the organization meets component parts of the various criteria. What follows is an analysis of selected components of the Sterling Criteria in each category and examples of what the principal should do in order to meet each of the selected criteria. These examples are not offered as a comprehensive plan for Sterling standard compliance, but rather as a demonstration of how well the skills of the Five Essentials facilitate the meeting of the Sterling Criteria. *The questions posed in each Sterling category are reprinted here with permission from The Florida Sterling Council.*

Leadership

Among other questions asked in the Leadership category of the Sterling system, the following two questions are particularly relevant to the Five Essentials:

1.   How do senior leaders establish and reinforce an environment for empowerment and innovation, and encourage and support organizational and employee learning (2000, p. 7)?

Clearly, the environment created by the elements of collaborative leadership produces the climate required by this criterion. The characteristics reflective of this climate include mutual trust, open mindedness, tolerance of divergent ideas, a tolerance for ambiguity, and the patience and skill to listen empathetically. Senior leaders must convince those around them that they have made a personal commitment to support and encourage innovation among staff members. Moreover, the senior leadership is in the position to either truly empower those around them or to thwart the efforts at empowerment by others. Senior leaders must be totally committed to the collaborative leadership efforts for this Sterling requirement to be met.

Building principals must not only learn the skills necessary to meet this Sterling requirement, they must also make a personal commitment to applying them on a daily basis. Establishing an environment for empowering stakeholders and encouraging innovation requires time and effort on the part of the building principal. Meeting the requirements for support of employee and organizational learning requires that the building principal restructure the organization and reallocate resources. Time needed for these efforts must be built into the school day. Building principals must learn to think differently about time and resource allocation. This all requires the development of new skills. The Five Essentials provide the necessary tools to accomplish this development. In order for building principals to "establish and reinforce an environment for empowerment and innovation, and encourage and support organizational and employee learning (2000, p. 7)," the building principal should

1. Practice collaborative leadership skills on a daily basis. By sharing power, the principal empowers employees.

2. Practice public engagement skills on a daily basis.

3. Share information and thereby empower employees.

4. Use conjoining conversation techniques to develop possible initiatives needed to improve learning or solve problems with the staff. Decide on possible initiatives by consensus.

2. How do senior leaders use organizational performance review findings and employee feedback to systematically improve their leadership effectiveness and the effectiveness of management throughout the organization (2000, p. 7)?

Trust is the singularly most important factor in the determination of authentic feedback regarding the performance of senior leadership as well as organizational effectiveness. Leadership earns trust by establishing a credible record of behavior in the eyes of the stakeholders. Feedback for senior leadership performance as well as organizational effectiveness should be welcomed on an autonomous basis. One of the most telling reflections of leadership effectiveness is to observe the degree of comfort with which stakeholders provide constructive criticism of leadership.

Building principals must develop personal confidence in their ability to learn and grow on the job to the degree that they can comfortably and openly share feedback with the stakeholders regarding organizational performance. Nothing is more invitational for stakeholders to become comfortable themselves in openly sharing changes they should make, based on feedback from other stakeholders, than the modeling of this activity by building principals. In order to "use organizational performance review findings and employee feedback to systematically improve their leadership effectiveness and the effectiveness of management throughout the organization (2000, p. 7)" the building principal should

1. Establish a school performance review team composed of representation from all stakeholders and employing the principles of public engagement and collaborative leadership.

2. Develop a school performance review survey and administer it autonomously to the school performance review team.

3. Collate the results of the performance review instrument and communicate these results to all stakeholders.

4. Develop from these review findings a listing of critical issues and forward it to the appropriate strategic action teams for consideration

and possible incorporation into current or newly created strategic objectives.

Strategic Planning

All four of the questions asked in the category of Strategic Planning particularly underscore the need for the Five Essentials skills:

1.   How do you develop action plans that address your key strategic objectives (2000, p. 10)?

Through training in collaborative leadership skills as well as public engagement principles, we can maximize the effectiveness of the action plan teams to meet the requirements of the district mission. Who we involve in the action plan teams and the manner in which the action teams operate should be governed by the principles of collaboration and stakeholder engagement.

For building principals, the school vision, compatible with the district mission, sets the parameters for action plans. In order to develop action plans within these parameters, the building principal should

a. Form multiple action teams based on each strategic objective. Membership on these teams should be representative of all stakeholders.

b. Provide training for all team members in collaborative leadership and the principles of public engagement. Specifically focus upon the principles of shared decision making.

c. Model through his/her behavior the principles of collaborative leadership and public engagement in shared decision making.

d. Utilize conjoining conservation techniques to reach consensus in all decision making with these teams.

e. Apply with the action teams the principles learned regarding public engagement and collaborative leadership to develop action plans with accompanying performance measures.

2.   How do you allocate resources to ensure accomplishment of your overall action plans (2000, p. 10)?

It is important to plan first and then allocate resources to that plan. Before we develop the budget, we develop the action plans called for in the strategy, which was in turn developed to help accomplish the mission. Before we look for new resources, we must reallocate from areas of spending that do *not* reflect current needs to areas the plan has targeted.

For building principals, the first order of business in this context is to reallocate current resources to align with the action plans. Second, he or she should explore the possibilities for outside funding. In order to accomplish this reallocation, the building principal should work with a shared decision-making team as follows:

a. Form a human and material resource allocation team composed of representatives of all stakeholders and operating with the principles of public engagement and collaborative leadership.

b. Utilizing this team, prioritize action plans based upon alignment with the school vision and all applicable strategic objectives.

c. Facilitate the team determination of current school spending outside the parameters of the school vision.

d. Reallocate these funds to be appropriated to meet the dollar requirements of the action plans through team decision making.

e. Facilitate the development of outside funding sources with this team.

3.   How do you communicate and deploy your strategic objectives, action plans, and performance measures/indicators to achieve overall organizational alignment (2000, p. 10)?

Once the strategic objectives, action plans, and performance measures/indicators are developed, the organization must deploy and align these elements of the strategic plan by redeploying resources of the organization. The resources of the organization must be targeted where necessary to accomplish these elements of the strategic plan. The stakeholders of the organization should be engaged in these decisions to both redeploy these resources and communicate these plans to the school/community.

The building principal must organize a communication and deployment plan reflecting the realignment of the organization to achieve the strategic objectives, action plans, and high performance results. This plan should be communicated to both the professional staff and the community. In order to accomplish this, he or she should

a. Establish an organizational alignment team representative of all stakeholders, trained in public engagement and collaborative leadership.

b. Review and analyze the current "alignment" of the school organization.

c. Facilitate team decision making regarding redesign of work units such as grade level and subject area departments, in order to create cross-functional teams more capable of successfully implementing action plans, strategic objectives, and performance indicators.

    d. Develop a plan to communicate to the professional staff and community realignment of the school organization to accommodate successful achievement of strategic objectives, action plans, and performance indicators.

    4. How does your projected performance compare with competitors, key benchmarks, and past performance, as appropriate? What is the basis for these comparisons (2000, p. 10)?

The basis for these comparisons is established first by the standards of excellence by which the organization governs itself. These standards of excellence represent, in a sense, the projected performance of the organization. The organization achieves excellence once all the standards are met. Areas for key benchmarking are determined by the standards of excellence, and the strategic plan presents the strategies to meet these benchmarks and eventually the standards as well. In addition, monitoring the implementation of the strategic plan tracks the progress of the performance of the organization. Benchmarking against competitors is included in the implementation of the Five Essentials. Collaborative decision-making during the strategic planning process incorporates both internal and external benchmarking.

The building principal must establish and present a basis for the comparison between projected performance and key benchmarks as well as past performance. In order to accomplish this, the building principal should

    a. Determine from the standards of excellence and action plans the expected student and organizational performance over the next three years relative to standardized testing data.

    b. Assemble comparable standardized student testing results from the last three years.

    c. Use internal and external benchmarking techniques in order to gather benchmarking data categorically comparable to student and organizational results targeted in the action plans and standards of excellence.

    d. Establish a tracking system to monitor results of numbers 1, 2, and 3 above.

    e. Utilize results of this tracking system to adjust and modify curriculum, instruction, and other organizational systems targeted in the strategic plan.

    f. Establish feedback intervals for staff and community regarding organizational performance.

Customer and Market Focus

This category examines how the "organization determines requirements, expectations, and preferences of its customers" (2000, p. 11).

1. How do you evaluate and improve your ability to know your customer requirements and use this information to develop improved product/service features (2000, p. 11)?

With full public engagement combined with collaborative leadership, the channels of conversation and feedback are open on a daily basis. The degree of trust generated by the implementation of the Five Essentials positions an organization to hear frank feedback regarding changes in service demands as well as current service areas in need of improvement. The evaluation of the ability of the organization to know customer requirements is best accomplished by the engagement of the public for this purpose. Both formal and informal evaluation of the organizational ability to know customer requirements can easily be sustained on a regular basis through discussions generated by the engagement of the public.

Principals gain "customer" knowledge through conversation. The practice of the principles of public engagement and collaborative leadership requires strong listening skills. In order to evaluate and improve their ability to learn stakeholder requirements and thereby develop improved educational services, principals should

a. Provide workshops on the development of strong listening skills in order to equip the professional staff to better understand parental concerns and complaints.

b. Assemble and periodically meet with a complaint and feedback team of parents respected by other parents for their reasonableness and honesty. Use the principles of public engagement and collaborative leadership to discuss and isolate areas of concerns and problems related to the delivery of school educational services.

c. Use parent complaints to understand possible breakdowns in the delivery of educational services.

d. Develop selection criteria based on standards of excellence to be used against issues revealed in complaints and concerns in order to screen legitimate breakdowns in the delivery of educational services.

e. Periodically apply the selection criteria developed in number 4 above to the collection of concerns and complaints registered in numbers 1, 2, and 3 above.

f. Make adjustments in the delivery of educational services based on the results of number 5 above.

2. What is your complaint management process? Include how you ensure that complaints are resolved effectively and promptly, and that all complaints received are aggregated and analyzed for use in overall organizational improvement (2000, p. 12).

Programs such as Kitchen Talk, School Block Talk, and Principal-Led Parental Collaboration should hold unattended complaints to a minimum. However, if you make public engagement and collaborative leadership a top priority, then job responsibilities must be realigned to include the resolution of complaints from beginning to end. In addition, the subjects for collaborative and engaged decision making should include strategic and policy considerations as a result of not meeting stakeholder needs.

Principals must be willing to place importance on parental feedback and complaints, especially those complaints upon which some positive action can be taken. In order to implement a complaint management process that can serve as a source for overall organizational improvement, the building principal should

a. Assemble the complaint and feedback team representing all stakeholders and practicing the principles of public engagement and collaborative leadership.

b. Facilitate with this team the development of a complaint management process that incorporates easy access, is designed to recover customer confidence, and is prompt and effective.

c. Develop a plan to communicate this complaint management process to the professional staff and community.

d. Compile complaint information from all sources and convene the complaint management team in order to evaluate implications of this data for organizational improvement.

e. Make organizational improvements in accordance with the results of number 4 above and communicate them to staff and community members.

Information and Analysis

The fourth category of the Sterling Criteria "examines your organization's performance measurement system and how your organization analyzes performance data and information" (2000, p. 13).

1.   How do you ensure that the results of organizational-level analysis are linked to work group and/or functional-level operations to enable effective support for decision making (2000, p. 14)?

Clearly, cross-functional teams serve the purpose of ensuring that those who analyze the data communicate it personally to those who use it to make appropriate adjustments and improvements.

The principles of shared decision making and collaborative leadership are important to this criterion because it demands support from work group and/or functional-level operations for decision making. In order to provide strategic and policy organizational-level analysis to work groups and/or functional-level operations, the building principal should

a. Utilizing the organization alignment team and employing shared decision making, develop a comprehensive organizational performance measurement system, focusing mainly on student achievement.

b. Communicate the organizational performance measurement plan to all stakeholders.

c. Track and communicate student achievement data to the professional staff on a weekly basis.

d. Communicate student achievement trends (improvement) to all stakeholders.

e. Provide a student achievement database to drive decisions regarding curricular and instructional changes.

f. Benchmark student achievement and curricular/instructional program performance against high performance and demographically comparable schools.

g. Communicate to all stakeholders improvement trends in student achievement data caused by organizational changes.

2.   How does analysis support daily operations throughout your organization? Include how this analysis ensures that measures align with action plans (2000, p. 14).

The Five Essentials may be employed effectively in the area of utilizing data analysis on several fronts. First, the strategic planning mission and strategies should direct the realignment of the responsibilities of the information analysts. Next, cross-functional teams should divide their agenda into two parts, strategic and operational. The agenda should deal with the strategies of the plan in the first instance and the daily implementation of the action plans in the second instance. In this manner, those using the data are in continuous communication with those preparing and analyzing the data.

It is the responsibility of the building principal to align strategies and action plans of the school with daily operations. In order to utilize assessment measures to support decisions about daily operations and guarantee alignment of action plans with these assessments, the principal should

a. Utilize the organization alignment team of stakeholders to develop assessment measures that reflect the substance of the action plans.

b. Utilize this team to apply these assessment measures against daily operations in order to isolate areas not congruent with the accomplishment of the action plans. To better align with the action plans, modify daily operations accordingly.

c. Communicate changes in daily operations to all professional staff.

Human Resource Focus

This category focuses on "how your organization enables employees to develop and utilize their full potential, aligned with the organization's objectives. Also examined are your organization's efforts to build and maintain a work environment and an employee support climate conducive to performance excellence, full participation, and personal and organizational growth" (2000, p. 15).

1.   How do you design, organize, and manage work and jobs to promote cooperation and collaboration, individual initiative, innovation, and flexibility, and to keep current with business needs (2000, p. 15)?

As described in Chapter 8, the cycle of implementation of the Five Essentials provides precisely what this Sterling Criterion requires. Training in the Five Essentials, particularly collaborative leadership and benchmarking for excellence, is designed to provide the kind of skills necessary to meet this requirement.

The building principal shoulders the responsibility to create the environment within his or her school that fosters cooperation and collaboration. The relationships between the principal and his or her staff members sets the cultural tone for his or her expectations regarding the importance of cooperation and collaboration among staff members. In order to create a school culture for staff that facilitates collaboration, cooperation, and innovation, the building principal should

a. Model the skills of the Five Essentials on a daily basis.

b. Set up ongoing training in the Five Essentials for both current and future staff members, utilizing the cycle of implementation of the Five Essentials (see Chapter 8).

c. Simplify job descriptions and create flexibility within performance indicators in order to encourage individual initiatives on the job.

d. Set up cross-functional instructional teams made up of differing Myers-Briggs Personality Types.

2. How do you ensure effective communication, cooperation, and knowledge/skill sharing across work units, functions, and locations, as appropriate (2000, p. 15)?

Interdepartmental cross-functional teams should examine current organizational strategies regarding effective communication, cooperation, knowledge, and skill sharing throughout the organization. Effective communication requires the sharing of information. However, most school organizations experience communication breakdown either through a lack of communication or through too much information being communicated, sometimes referred to as "data overload." As suggested in Chapter 3, "Benchmark for Excellence," it becomes the responsibility of cross-functional teams to develop selection criteria through which to filter all the information gathered, in order to communicate to the appropriate members of the organization the intelligence to improve the delivery of services for which they are directly responsible. The application of the skills of benchmarking as well as those developed through collaborative leadership practices produce team cooperation and communication of best practices throughout the organization.

Fundamental changes in the focus of staff development programs are required to develop the skills necessary to ensure effective communication across school organizations. In order to ensure effective communication and cooperative skill development across school staffs, principals should

a. Recognize that communication is an important skill necessary to high performance organizations.

b. Train all staff in the skills of collaborative leadership and public engagement.

c. Ensure that the performance-assessment information flow supports individual and group high performance for both staff and student.

d. Initiate ongoing training in the Five Essentials for all incoming staff members.

3. How do you seek and use input from employees and their supervisors and managers on education and training needs, expectations, and design (2000, p. 16)?

Input gained through strategic planning utilizing collaborative decision-making skills combined with stakeholder engagement in the process creates the organizational ability to develop the most appropriate design to meet the organizational education and training needs. Once the design of the delivery of education and training is developed, it is through the engagement of the organizational stakeholders in ongoing collaborative dialogue that the education and training needs are updated almost on a daily basis.

Rapidly changing demands of the workplace require workforce development programs that produce the skills necessary for high performance in a constantly changing organization. In order for building principals to know and address education and training needs of their teachers and other staff members, they should

a. Determine, through shared decision making with the school staff, skills required by the strategic action plans.

b. Determine, through shared decision-making with the school staff, training needs in order to develop skills required by the action plans but currently lacking in the staff.

c. Design a staff development program aligned with the strategic action plans of the school and utilizing the results of 1 and 2 above.

Process Management

This category "examines the key aspects of your organization's process management, including customer focused design, product and service delivery, support, and supplier and partnering processes involving all work units" (2000, p. 18).

1. How do your design processes address design quality and cycle time (2000, p. 18)?

This represents an area in need of improvement in American schools today. In Chapter 6, I discussed the quality assurance program associated with governing by standards. For all standards of excellence (including, for example, Standard 3.1, Plan of the Curriculum) the quality assurance program will flush a lack of quality defined as not complying with the appropriate standard. Again, benchmarking externally for best practices on the plan of the curriculum, for example, provides the opportunity for school organizations to develop intelligence specific to their own standards and relevant needs.

Building principals must insure that changing student needs are addressed in the curricular/instructional program. Particularly, they must provide for the development of curricular and/or instructional changes or additions that meet changing student needs. In addition, the plan of the curriculum should also address timely response from the point of development of the new curriculum to the point of operational implementation. Every job level and department affected by this change must be well informed in order to avoid problems caused by time and coordination delays due to a lack of effective communication of the curricular changes. In order to ensure that "design processes address design quality and cycle time" (2000, p. 18), the building principal should

    a. Analyze the plan of the curriculum in order to ensure that the Plan of the Curriculum Standard of Excellence includes clearly delineated criteria of quality, timeliness of response to changes, and coordination of changes through all job levels affected by the implementation of any curricular changes.

    b. Make changes in the plan of the curriculum where discrepancies are found in number 1 above.

    c. Communicate any changes in number 2 above to all stakeholders.

    2.   What are your design processes for products and services and their related production and delivery processes (2000, p. 18)?

Public schools need to spend more time and energy on the design and delivery of programs and services that reflect emerging needs of students and parents. The design process for public school organizations should incorporate (1) the intelligence from both internal and external benchmarking; (2) input from collaborative discussions with the public, including parents; (3) alignment with the standards of excellence; and (4) alignment with the strategic plan, all of which are outlined in "Student Results Benchmarking" in Chapter 3.

Again, building principals need to be skilled in collaborative leadership, benchmarking, and strategic planning. These skills are required in order to develop educational programs and services that meet and anticipate student needs in an ongoing fashion. In order to ensure that the design processes for the development of educational services and the delivery of these services by schools reflect changing student requirements, coordination of their delivery across the professional staff, and quality performance requirements, principals should

    a. Establish a student needs assessment team representative of all stakeholders to review and project, using public engagement principles, student needs.

    b. Using the results from number 1 above to establish screening criteria, benchmark externally to establish quality performance standards for new educational programs.

c. Align and coordinate the implementation of new educational programs with the responsibilities of the professional staff and communicate this to all stakeholders.

Business Results

This Sterling category "examines your organization's performance and improvement in key business areas—customer satisfaction, product and service performance, financial and marketplace performance, human resource results, supplier and partner results, and operational performance" (2000, p. 22).

1.   What are your current levels and trends in key measures and/or indicators of customer satisfaction, dissatisfaction, and satisfaction relative to competitors (2000, p. 22)?

Public engagement targeted at collaborative discussions regarding external benchmarking intelligence satisfies this requirement. Open and full discussions with the public regarding programs and services offered by recognized high-performing school districts provides a basis for comparisons. This positions the school district to allocate resources accordingly and in keeping with their strategic plan.

Principals must facilitate the process of public engagement to determine public satisfaction with the educational services of the school. In order to establish the current levels and trends in key indicators of parental satisfaction, the principal should

a. Utilize the complaint and feedback team representative of all stakeholders and employ the principles of public engagement and collaborative leadership. Review with this team the most recent findings of the quality restoration team from the governance model (Chapter 6). Compile a list of specific areas reported by the quality restoration team but not yet in compliance with standards.

b. Review with this team complaints and concerns not yet resolved.

c. Review with this team school awards and recognitions from independent organizations and local agencies.

d. Compile and administer, with this team, a parental satisfaction survey to all parents of school students.

e. Compile the results from numbers 1, 2, 3, and 4 above.

f. Communicate with all stakeholders the trends and key indicators found in number 5 above.

2.   What are your current levels and trends in key measures and/or indicators of employee well-being, satisfaction and dissatisfaction, and deployment (2000, p. 24)?

Again, employee-management teams practicing collaborative decision making produces the indicators of employee satisfaction. More importantly, utilizing the skills required by the implementation of collaborative leadership practiced by all the stakeholders will produce high levels of employee satisfaction.

Building principals need to practice the skills of collaborative leadership with employee-management teams in an ongoing fashion. Shared decision making helps create the environment within the school that facilitates employee gratification and satisfaction. In order to establish "current levels and trends in key measures and/or indicators of employee satisfaction and dissatisfaction, and deployment (2000, p. 24)," the building principal should

a. Establish an employee-management team composed of teachers and other staff members and utilizing the principles of collaborative leadership.

b. Review with this team employee complaints not yet resolved.

c. With this team, compile and administer an employee satisfaction survey to all school employees.

d. Compile the results from numbers 2 and 3 above.

e. Communicate with all school employees the trends and key indicators found in number 4 above.

The skills of the Five Essentials play a critical role in facilitating the process of meeting the Sterling Criteria. In the search for excellence in both organizational performance and student achievement, the skills of the Five Essentials equip all the stakeholders to maximize their individual contribution to the accomplishment of strategic objectives as well as peak daily performance.

The culture nurtured by the interaction of stakeholders equipped with the skills of the Five Essentials maximizes the opportunity for student learning. Furthermore, this environment becomes self-sustaining as the development of these skills becomes ongoing.

WHAT DRIVES ORGANIZATIONS TO STERLING EXCELLENCE?

According to The Florida Sterling Council, the Sterling Criteria for Organizational Performance Excellence, "are built upon a set of core values and concepts. These values and concepts are the foundation for integrating key business requirements within a results-oriented framework (2000, p. vii)." Many organizations, public schools in particular, lack the skills in their workforce to meet the rigorous human resource requirements of performance excellence such as those demanded by the Sterling Criteria or the Baldrige Quality System.

The human resource requirements of the Sterling Core Values and Performance Criteria underscore the importance of training in the Five Essentials to school transformation. The skills acquired by such training produce precisely the talent required to meet the demands of the Sterling System.

Figure 7.1 depicts the integration of the Sterling Core Values with the Five Essentials. There is a very close match between what is required by the Sterling Core Values and the skills that training in the Five Essentials produces. Therefore, training in the Five Essentials will drive an organization toward Sterling-defined excellence.

STERLING CORE VALUES

The Sterling Core Values and Concepts are the foundation for the Sterling Criteria for Organizational Performance Excellence. The Sterling Core Values are reprinted here with permission from The Florida Sterling Council (2000, p. vii). These core values and the integration of the Five Essentials with them are as follows:

Customer-Driven Quality

Public engagement facilitates the attainment of excellence. Parents engaged in feedback on the delivery of school services provide the opportunity to make modifications in a timely and more effective manner. With parents involved in collaborative decision making, the Sterling requirement for "constant sensitivity to changing and emerging customer and market requirements"(2000, p. vii) is more effectively met. Over the years, much of the resistance of school districts to changing parent and student needs was experienced as a result of the "we, they" mentality created by traditional and hierarchical school organizations. Local resistance to state and federal mandates regarding special education serves as a good example of unnecessary acrimony and confrontation between schools and the stakeholders they serve. It is important to note that engaging the public in decision making regarding school programs and policies carries with it a partnership that shares, to some degree, the responsibility for the effectiveness of the organization. When combined wisdom of the stakeholders of schools today replaces the confrontation between parents and school leaders of yesterday, schools are more likely to realize their full potential.

Leadership

Sterling requires that, "An organization's senior leaders need to set directions and create a customer orientation, clear and visible values, and high expectations" (2000, p. vii). Developing the skills of the Five

Figure 7.1 Five Essentials Integrated With Sterling Core Values

Core Values Sterling

Five Essentials

	Public Engagement	Planning Strategically	Govern by Standards	Benchmark for Excellence	Lead Collaboratively
Customer Driven Quality	Constant Parent Feedback			Benchmark Against Competition	
Leadership	Stakeholders engaged collaboratively to set direction	Stakeholders engaged to strategize for excellence	Standards of Excellence guide all decisions		Build Stake-Holder Skills through Collaboration
Continuous Improvement and Learning	Feedback for improvement from public engagement			Best Practices & Benchmarking	
Valuing Employees	Conversation Circles, Establish Training Needs	Five Essentials Training	Align Training with skills req'd By Standards of Excellence		Establish Training Needs-Conversation Circles
Fast Response	Parent Feedback on Response Time	Simplify work process through mission alignment	Align Process Management with Standards of Excellence	Benchmark on High Performing Response Time	
Design Quality & Prevention	Meaningful impact on Program Design	Analysis of weaknesses guides needed program designs	Design programs to align with Standards of Excellence	Benchmark against High Performing Program Designs	
Long Range View of the Future		Develop & Implement			
Management by Fact				Information filtered into local intelligence	
Partnership Development	University & Labor/Management Partnerships Engaged				Cross Functional Teams
Public Responsibility & Citizenship			Standards demand more than mere compliance		
Results Focus	Results focus is on Student Achievement. The cycle of Implementation of the Five Essentials is administered across all Sterling Criteria on a continuous basis.				

Reprinted with permission from the Florida Sterling Council, pp. vii–x.

Essentials empowers the stakeholders to invest personally in an effort to help "set" directions"(2000, p. vii) of the organization and to do so effectively. Moreover, the responsibility for setting directions should not fall exclusively on the shoulders of senior leadership. This important function becomes a collaborative enterprise for stakeholders trained in the Five Essentials, and the role of senior leadership becomes that of facilitator.

Continuous Improvement and Learning

"Achieving the highest levels of performance requires a well-executed approach to continuous improvement and learning" (2000, p. vii). As mentioned earlier, engaging the public (parents) offers the best approach to gathering input from the public. With training in Benchmarking for Excellence and Engaging the Public, these activities easily become a "regular part of daily work" (2000, p. vii). Benchmarking and incorporating best practices "at individual, work unit, and organizational levels" (2000, p. vii) is inherent in the implementation of the Five Essentials.

Valuing Employees

This requirement of Sterling is met by the skills of the Five Essentials as follows:

Engage the public in conversation circles to determine training needs;

Plan strategically to train the stakeholders in the skills of the Five Essentials;

Align the training with the skills required by the standards of excellence; and

Establish training needs through collaborative decision making with staff.

Fast Response

This requirement stipulates, "Major improvements in response time often require simplification of work units and processes (2000, p. viii). Work processes from the past must be currently justified by alignment to the organizational mission. Failing to so align, they should be abandoned. Work processes should profile a consistency with the strategic plan. Action plans from the strategic plan should point the way to simplifying work processes. Benchmarking on high performance response time facilitates the development of streamlined work processes. Finally, the work processes should align with the standards of excellence.

Design Quality and Prevention

This component of the Sterling Core Values and Concepts draws upon the skills of all Five Essentials. Collaborative discussions with the public produce a meaningful impact on program design. Also making an impact is the analysis of strengths and weaknesses from the process of strategic planning. Organizational benchmarking through cross-functional teams enhances "the ability to use information from diverse sources and data bases that combine findings involving customer preferences" (2000, p. viii). This in turn improves design quality. Finally, the organizational programs should be designed to align with standards of excellence.

Long Range View of the Future

This category of the Sterling core values requires a quality process of strategic planning and commitment to the stakeholders that contemplates changing customer needs and changing demographics (2000, pp. viii–ix). Strategic planning, when combined with the other four essentials, enables organizations to meet this core value. Moreover, there is a responsibility to the public that must be reflected in the mission and operation of the school district. Certainly, public schools must take this responsibility very seriously. Relying upon a staff that possess and practices the skills of the Five Essentials positions a school to excel at meeting this responsibility.

Management by Fact

This category requires that an organization utilizes measures of performance that best represent the factors that lead to improved customer and operational performance. It also requires multiple measures of performance. Further, it demands that "data and analysis support a variety of purposes, such as planning, reviewing overall performance, improving operations, and comparing performance with competitors or with 'best practices' benchmarks" (2000, p. ix).

In each of these requirements, the training in the Five Essentials provides the needed processes and workforce skills. Feedback from the stakeholders, student achievement data, and the evaluation of compliance with standards of excellence provide multiple measures of organizational performance. Benchmarking, both internally and externally, provides intelligence with which to polish best practices. In addition, strategic planning provides multiple measurement indicators throughout the organization.

Partnership Development

This category requires that the organization enter into partnership to help them better accomplish their goals (2000, p. ix). Schools have been involved in partnerships for some years now. However, these partnerships need to be targeted to align with the overall organizational goals. Engaging the public and utilizing cross-functional teams in a collaborative manner should produce the best strategy for forming partnerships beneficial to achieving the organizational goals and objectives.

Public Responsibility and Citizenship

This category calls for the organization leadership "to stress its responsibilities to the public" (2000, p. ix). It further requires that, "Organizations should not only meet all . . . laws and regulatory requirements, they should treat these and related requirements as opportunities for continuous improvement beyond mere compliance" (2000, p. ix). Incorporating these civic responsibilities into an organization's standards of excellence allows it to demand more than just compliance with laws and regulatory requirements. Engaging the public in a collaborative manner guarantees compliance with this core value. High-performing school organizations skilled in the Five Essentials become pace setters and perform well above a basic compliance standard.

Results Focus

This category requires that "an organization's performance measurements need to focus on key results. Results should be focused on creating and balancing value for all stakeholders" (2000, p. x). For school organizations, the primary results focus and performance measurement is student achievement. This focus applies across all grade levels and stakeholders. This performance measurement is also the primary benchmark that fuels the cycle of implementation of the Five Essentials.

Engaging the public in meaningful decision making helps strike a healthy balance in meeting diverse needs of all stakeholders. Practicing the skills of collaborative leadership facilitates working through tough and sometimes conflicting issues and opinions to a fruitful conclusion.

The Five Essentials for transforming schools facilitate meeting the Sterling Criteria for Organizational Performance Excellence as well as the Sterling Core Values. As the cycle of implementation of the Five Essentials is applied on a continuing basis, the Five Essentials focus the energy and resources of the organization in such a manner that the Sterling core values and performance criteria are met.

SUMMARY

The Florida Sterling Criteria for Organizational Performance Excellence aligns with the Five Essentials for the transformation of schools. The core values of this system are very similar to the Five Essentials. Such categories as Leadership, Strategic Planning, and Customer and Market Focus align with similar areas of the Five Essentials.

When we focus on the specific areas examined by the Sterling system, we find that the Five Essentials, and the skills associated with them, empower educational organizations to meet the Sterling requirements. In this chapter, we applied the Five Essentials to the Sterling system and found there was indeed a very good match. In addition, we examined the core values of the Sterling system and again found that the Five Essentials and the skills associated with them met these Sterling requirements.

Not only do the Five Essentials integrate well with the demands of the Sterling system, they integrate well with each other. *How* well is the subject of the next chapter.

8

Integrate the Five Essentials

During the last few years, a new understanding of the process of organizational change has emerged. It is not top-down or bottom-up, but participative at all levels—aligned through common understanding of a system.

—Peter Senge et al. (1994)

SIMULTANEOUS DEVELOPMENT

The transformation of a school or school district into a learning organization relies upon simultaneous organizational development. None of the Five Essentials should be viewed or implemented in isolation. The strength of the overlapping and connecting concepts among the essentials is their most empowering transformation tool, as the power of one of the essentials can be harnessed in the implementation of another. Public school organizations that approach comprehensive reform in a linear fashion are doomed to failure. The mechanistic and monodimensional character of linear reform efforts typically do not contemplate nor incorporate the multidimensional character of effective working relationships among the organizational stakeholders. Successful organizational development requires understanding the fundamental quality of relationships to be developed among the stakeholders.

The integration of the Five Essentials can easily happen at all strategic and operational levels of a school district. With a little experience utilizing these concepts, there develops a natural flow and rhythm to the process. Integrating the Five Essentials is illustrated by the following example and also in Figure 8.1:

The number of high school dropouts has escalated in school district A. Over the past five years, it has increased from five percent to nine percent. The school board has charged the administration to make a recommendation regarding how to solve the problem.

The recommendation to the school board should indicate the thoughts and meanings supporting it. It should reflect the results of applying conjoining conversation techniques to the problem and reaching consensus on its definition, analysis, and major causes. Alternative solutions should be included in the recommendation, along with an evaluation of the congruency of these solutions with the district mission and pertinent local standards of excellence. The best solution should be recommended, along with aids and impediments to implementation. The final action plan should include specific steps to be taken.

The Five Essentials, when working simultaneously, help develop an atmosphere of trust and sharing. Many traditional administrators will put forth the argument that people are quick to provide their input on any number of issues, but when *you* are responsible for the final decision, it is *you* and you alone who will be held accountable for the impact of that decision. However, shared decision making incorporated into the Five Essentials leads to shared credit, responsibility, and authority.

Twenty or thirty years ago, the position of public school management at the bargaining table was hard and fast on such issues as "fair dismissal" and "reduction in force." Their position was characterized as a management right, and there was in management's view no rationale for including these issues in a labor contract. What we have since learned is that it is far easier to implement a reduction in force when the guidelines have already been agreed to by those affected. "All-party ownership" of these issues has replaced the confrontational "us against them" of earlier years.

One of the major common elements of the Five Essentials is that they all require meaning to be found in conversation among and between the stakeholders of the school district. In *The Fifth Discipline Fieldbook*, Peter Senge et al. (1994) point out that,

> Many members of the organization . . . have a collective sense of its underlying purpose. . . this shared sense of purpose is often tacit . . . To become more aware of the organization's purpose, ask the members of the organization and learn to listen for the answers. (p. 299)

Figure 8.1 Cross-Functional Action Plan to Solve Dropout Problem

Action	Essential Element Category	Category of Individuals
Engage stakeholders affected by or affecting the problem Establish cross-functional team	Public Engagement Strategic Planning	High school teachers, Pupil personnel administrators, High School Principals, Parents, Parents of dropouts, Curriculum supervisors, Students
State the problem utilizing conjoining conversation	Collaborative Leadership	Conjoining conversation facilitator and Cross-Functional Team
Gather pertinent data from other high schools known to have excellent dropout prevention programs	Benchmark for Excellence	Parents, teachers, administrators from other high schools
Gather pertinent internal data	Benchmark for Excellence	Parents, Teachers, Administrators, Curriculum Supervisors
Compare dropout problem against district mission and standard of excellence, standard 3.1 Plan of Curriculum, & Review Evaluation of Graduates	Govern by Standards Strategic Planning	Cross-functional team School Board members
Draft action plan Recommendation to school board	Strategic Planning Benchmark for Excellence Govern by Standards Lead Collaboratively Public Engagement	Cross-functional Team

As previously discussed, Stephen Covey, in *The Seven Habits of Highly Effective People* (1989, p. 240), speaks to specific requirements of listening. He asserts, "When I say empathic listening, I mean *seeking first* to understand, to really understand." He goes on to say, "Empathic (from *empathy*) listening gets inside another person's frame of reference. You look out through it, you see the world the way they see the world, you understand their paradigm, you understand how they feel." As Senge et al. suggest, when you learn to listen to stakeholders speak of the purpose of their organization, it is important to practice empathic listening as Covey describes it.

As we discussed earlier concerning the Nine Factors of public engagement, we must recognize that people do not form relationships with public institutions without emotion. There is an energy created by the emotion surrounding the problems and issues facing public schools today.

THE CYCLE OF IMPLEMENTATION OF THE FIVE ESSENTIALS

Implementation of the Five Essentials will not happen overnight. It is important to note that one should not be implemented in isolation from the others. Their nature is an interrelated one. However, the Five Essentials do lend themselves to stages of implementation. The following scenario assumes that none of the Five Essentials has a prevalent presence in the operation of the school district.

The model found in Figure 8.2 represents the implementation of the Five Essentials, from beginning discussions and training to full implementation.

Stage 1—Process

It is important to train a combination of the various stakeholders in the fundamental concepts of the Five Essentials. Cohort groups of 30 participants drawn from teachers, administrators, and community members provide the proper mix of differing perspectives that enables the application of the skills of the Five Essentials to produce the combined wisdom of all the participants. This training marks the beginning of the local leadership academy that will become a major vehicle of the human resource development division of the school district.

Training at this stage represents an initial commitment to the Five Essentials. Participants should be given the opportunity to engage in conversation with one another in both formal and informal exchanges. The content should focus on institutional and individual topics and concerns. The following is an outline of the Stage 1 training:

COLLABORATIVE LEADERSHIP

1. Administer and discuss the Collaborative Leadership Survey

2. Discuss and practice the impact of effective conversation

Figure 8.2 Implementation of the Five Essentials

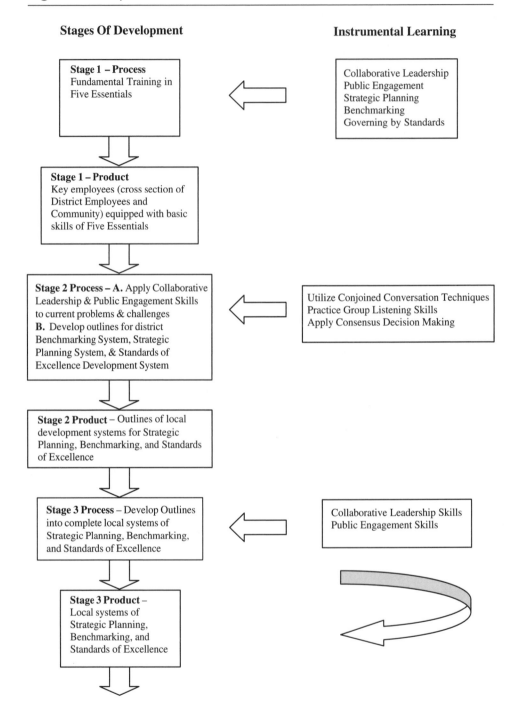

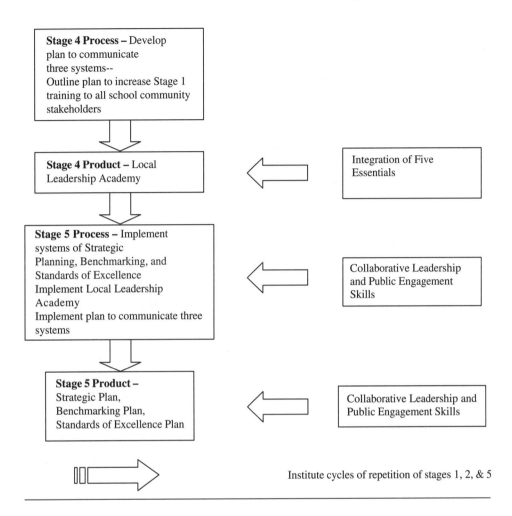

3. Illustrate and practice "defining the problem or challenge"

4. Develop steps for building trust in the organization

5. Define and illustrate the value of cross-functional teams

6. Discuss and practice the concept of "shared power"

7. Compare and contrast traditional leadership versus collaborative leadership

8. Develop understanding of "systems thinking" in the context of collaborative leadership.

The Collaborative Leadership Training should be tailored to the individual needs of each school or school district. The results of the collaborative leadership survey will point the way to areas that will need more training time, attention, and development than others.

PUBLIC ENGAGEMENT

1. Administer the Public Engagement Survey

2. Review and apply exercises from the Nine Factors of Public Engagement, from the research of The Kettering Foundation entitled *Meaningful Chaos, How People Form Relationships with Public Concerns*

3. Use conjoining conversation techniques (see Chapter 1) with participants to develop a list of current and local controversial issues

4. Contrast traditional practice with the practice of public engagement

5. Develop an outline of solutions to controversial issues utilizing practices of public engagement.

Public Engagement Training should focus on team building and the development of trust.

STRATEGIC PLANNING

1. Administer the Strategic Planning Survey

2. Develop understanding of mission statement, strategies, and action plans

3. Develop understanding of the relationship of the other four essentials to the strategic planning process

4. Explain and illustrate the concept of redeployment of district resources to empower the strategic plan

5. Prioritize the most pressing needs of the school or school district.

Strategic Planning Training should focus on the value of using the other four essentials in the development of the strategic plan. The plan itself will not become part of the everyday operation of the school district without stakeholders employing the skills of the other four essentials.

BENCHMARKING FOR EXCELLENCE

1. Administer Benchmarking Survey

2. Review and explain the Sterling Criteria for Organizational Performance Excellence

3. Explain and illustrate the relationship of the Sterling Criteria to benchmarking

4. Review identification of "best practices"

5. Define and explain "public school intelligence"

6. Use conjoining conversation techniques to identify strengths and weaknesses of school or school district

7. Define and illustrate the Quality Assurance Program

8. Examine weaknesses of the school or school district in the context of the Sterling Criteria for Organizational Performance Excellence.

This training provides benchmarking and competitive intelligence as a means to achieve excellence in student learning.

GOVERNING BY STANDARDS

1. Administer the Standards of Excellence Survey

2. Explain the governance model

3. Review and illustrate the standards of excellence in the basic program areas of school board, human resources and instructional services, curricular and pupil personnel services, and educational program design and special education services

4. Review and explain compliance with standards of excellence

5. Review and explain quality restoration services.

Governing by standards requires consensus decision making at every step of the process.

Stage 1—Product

The result of the Stage 1 training is of course a cross section of stakeholders trained in the skills of the Five Essentials. In order to begin to apply these skills to improvement efforts in the school or school district, it is important to first proceed in areas of need that are more easily improved than in the more challenging areas. As these stakeholders practice their newly acquired skills, their skills will improve. Stage 2 is designed to provide these kinds of opportunities while making a contribution to the ongoing efforts to improve the school or school district.

Stage 2—Process

A. Once the first group of stakeholders is trained, it is important to provide opportunities for those trained to immediately put these skills to work for the school or school district. Collaborative leadership and public engagement skills should be initially applied to the more easily understood problems and challenges. The skills of collaborative leadership and public engagement both rely upon the ability of the problem solvers to listen deeply and come to a common meaning. The major objective of this part of the training is not to solve the problems but rather to polish the skills of the stakeholders.

B. After the stakeholders have been trained and given the opportunity to apply these skills , outlines for systems of benchmarking, strategic planning, and the development of standards of excellence are produced by the trained stakeholders. These outlines are tailored to fit the individual needs of the school or school district.

Stage 2—Product

The product of the Stage 2 Process is three well-constructed outlines for systems of benchmarking, strategic planning, and the development of standards of excellence. These outlines are tailor-made for the school or school district by stakeholders with a personal investment in the success of the organization. This represents an important strength of the cycle of implementation. As stakeholders learn the skills of the Five Essentials, they apply them to the development of systems reflecting the unique needs and goals of their organization.

Stage 3—Process

In the third stage, the outlines for the locally developed systems of strategic planning, benchmarking, and standards of excellence are used to produce complete plans. The following is a list of considerations that should be addressed as these outlines take on form and substance:

1. Necessary further human resources training

2. Necessary redeployment of human and material resources

3. Current administrative arrangements that must be changed

4. Alignment of job responsibilities and Five Essentials systems

5. Necessary budgeting changes

6. Necessary governance board policy changes to align policy with Five Essentials systems.

7. Necessary waivers of union contracts not aligned with Five Essentials systems.

Stage 3—Product

The output of the Stage 3 process is a combination of three locally developed systems, strategic planning, benchmarking, and standards of excellence, for the governance board to adopt. However, before these systems are implemented, Stages 4 and 5 should be completed.

Stage 4—Process

At this point, a plan to communicate these three systems should be developed, which should include a "road show" that takes the integrated essentials to all school community stakeholders. The communication of these systems should engage the stakeholders in dialogue about them.

A plan to expand Stage 1 training to all school community stakeholders should also be developed. This plan will, of necessity, pay special attention to the redeployment of the human resources considered in the strategic planning process and Stage 3 considerations.

Stage 4—Product

The result of the Stage 4 efforts is a local leadership academy and a plan to communicate the three essential systems of strategic planning, benchmarking, and standards of excellence.

Stage 5—Process

During Stage 5, the local systems of strategic planning, benchmarking, and standards of excellence are implemented, along with the plan to communicate these systems. Finally, the local leadership academy is fully implemented. The momentum from these efforts will grow quickly. The need for the stakeholders to be engaged will be given a productive channel and a meaningful opportunity for all who wish to be involved.

Stage 5—Product

The outcome of the implementations of Stage 5, once completed, is a strategic plan, a benchmarking plan, and a governance plan incorporating standards of excellence.

Once this cycle of system development and implementation is completed, Stages 1 and 2 should be considered as ongoing in order to orient and train the stakeholders as the school or school district establishes a continuous improvement profile.

COST–BENEFIT ANALYSIS

As in the private sector, school organizations should submit proposed improvements to a cost-benefit analysis. The criteria against which to measure the benefit can be found in the standards of excellence from the governance program (see Chapter 6). Questions to ask would include, Does the proposed benefit help the attainment of a standard with which the organization is currently not in compliance? Is it compatible with the mission? Is the cost proportional to the measure of the need for which this benefit provides? Is it possible to redeploy resources from an area of the budget not currently serving the mission?

ADMINISTRATIVE ARRANGEMENTS VERSUS CURRICULAR CONCERNS

For years, public schools have established and maintained "administrative arrangements" to accommodate the administration of the schools. Many of these arrangements have become institutionalized over the years. In many cases, it does not seem to matter if they still serve the same purpose or need they were originally created to serve.

Administrative arrangements deal with "how" we organize for instruction in schools. High school schedules, grouping for instruction, the length of class periods, the length of the school day and year, and the school calendar are just a few examples. Changes in these deeply rooted arrangements happen rarely, and when they do, the reason for the change often has more to do with local or state politics than with "what is best" regarding learning opportunities for students.

JUSTIFY OR ELIMINATE

Without question, many of these administrative arrangements must be replaced with organizational structures that are compatible with the instructional strategies and curricular concerns given birth by the application of the skills of the Five Essentials. Policies as well as administrative arrangements should be justified on an annual basis, or they should be eliminated.

Because of a history of traditional administrative practice that assumes an underlying "we, they" mentality and reliance upon outdated policies, traditional decision making appears, at times, to be mindless and unresponsive to obvious and changed needs that are far better addressed by shared decision making. Although policies and rules are necessary, not every situation or set of circumstances can be contemplated when drafting such policies or rules using traditional administrative practices. In order to be more responsive to changing needs and circumstances, the needs of stakeholders, including students, are best addressed through their involvement in the decision making that ultimately affects them. Further, the combined wisdom produced by shared decision making develops mutual support for the decisions made by applying policies developed in this manner. Again, shared decision making offers a more effective, combined form of wisdom for such matters. In this way, mindfulness replaces apparent mindlessness.

SUMMARY

With simultaneous training and implementation, the Five Essentials work in concert with one another. This chapter was designed to provide a guide to develop and produce (1) training in the Five Essentials, (2) local systems of strategic planning, benchmarking, and standards development, (3) a local leadership development academy, and (4) a strategic plan, a benchmarking plan, and a governance program incorporating standards of excellence.

The skills of the Five Essentials empower the organizational stakeholders to work productively together to not only accomplish their organizational mission but also to achieve organizational performance excellence. How learning organizations can achieve organizational excellence by using lessons from chaos theory and how the Five Essentials relate to the "new science" are the subject of the next chapter.

9

Chaos, Essentials, and Learning Organizations

A self-organizing system has the freedom to grow and evolve, guided only by one rule: It must remain consistent with itself and its past.

—Margaret Wheatley (1992)

FIVE ESSENTIALS AND THE NEW SCIENCE

There is a new science of organizational form emerging with which the Five Essentials are compatible, because they are rooted in the same basic beliefs and concepts. This new science can be explained to some degree by looking to chaos theory.

INFORMATION, RELATIONSHIPS, AND CHAOS

Margaret Wheatley, in her book *Leadership and the New Science,* shares her views of learning about chaos that reveals order. She writes of a new way to lead organizations:

There is a simpler way to lead organizations. . . . I believe our present ways of understanding organizations are skewed. . . . The layers of complexity, the sense of things being beyond our control and out of control, are but signals of our failure to understand a deeper reality of organizational life. (1992, p. 3)

Clearly, Wheatley and others are committed to finding new and better ways—revolutionary ways—of understanding organizations and organizational life. Parallels to this enterprise are not difficult to find. Fritjof Capra, in his book *The Turning Point: Science, Society, and the Rising Culture*, speaks of a turning point in science as follows:

In the twentieth century, physicists faced, for the first time, a serious challenge to their ability to understand the universe. Every time they asked nature a question in an atomic experiment, nature answered with a paradox, and the more they tried to clarify the situation, the sharper the paradoxes became. In their struggle to grasp this new reality, scientists became painfully aware that their basic concepts, their language, and their whole way of thinking were inadequate to describe atomic phenomena. Their problem was not only intellectual but involved an intense emotional and existential experience. (1983, pp. 76–77)

What I have attempted to accomplish with my explanations and descriptions of the Five Essentials is to demonstrate how our basic concepts, language, and indeed our very way of thinking about school organizations are inadequate to understand their underlying needs and, more important, the needs of the relationships of their stakeholders. Just as Capra points out the inability of the science community to describe and understand atomic phenomena using ways of thinking that are inadequate to the task, so, too, are leaders of school organizations unable to rely upon traditional ways of organizing schools to explain and ultimately meet the challenges of a community and world that have grown far more diverse.

Not only have the communities served by public schools all over our nation grown more diverse, they have also developed far more sophisticated expectations from their schools. Relying upon thinking from the past regarding school organizational forms will not and has not produced the changes in these organizations required to meet the new and different elements of a more diverse constituency, reflecting the needs of what is becoming ultimately a new world order.

James Gleick, in his book *Chaos: Making a New Science* (1987), explains the concept of "mode locking," which may have some implications for school organizations:

Christian Huygens, the seventeenth-century Dutch physicist who helped invent both the pendulum clock and the classical science of dynamics . . . noticed one day that a set of pendulum clocks placed against a wall happened to be swinging in perfect chorus-line synchronization. He knew that the clocks could not be that accurate. Nothing in the mathematical description then available for a pendulum could explain this mysterious propagation of order from one pendulum to another. Huygens surmised, correctly, that the clocks were coordinated by vibrations transmitted through the wood. This phenomenon, in which one regular cycle locks into another, is now called entrainment, or mode locking. Mode locking explains why the moon always faces the earth, or more generally why satellites tend to spin in some whole-number ratio of their orbital period: 1 to 1, or 2 to 1, or 3 to 2. When the ratio is close to a whole number, nonlinearity in the tidal attraction of the satellite tends to lock it in. Mode locking occurs throughout electronics, making it possible, for example, for a radio receiver to lock in on signals even when there are small fluctuations in their frequency. . . . A spectacular example in nature is a Southeast Asian species of firefly that congregates in trees during mating periods, thousands at one time, blinking in a fantastic spectral harmony.

With all such control phenomena, a critical issue is robustness: how well can a system withstand small jolts. Equally critical in biological systems is flexibility: how well can a system function over a range of frequencies. A locking-in to a single mode can be enslavement, preventing a system from adapting to change. Organisms must respond to circumstances that vary rapidly and unpredictably; no heartbeat or respiratory rhythm can be locked into the strict periodicities of the simplest physical models, and the same is true of the subtler rhythms of the rest of the body. (pp. 292–293)

Is it possible that school organizations have experienced mode locking? Has this locking into a single mode of traditional organizational form prevented school systems from "adapting to change," as Gleick suggests for systems in general? No system has experienced the need for change more than school organizations. Is it possible that locking into a single mode has produced enslavement, preventing school organizations from initiating much-needed adaptations? Just as Gleick points out that organisms in general must respond to circumstances that vary rapidly and unpredictably, so must public school organizations. Traditional organizational forms have provided a mode locking environment that has enslaved public school organizations and their stakeholders in traditional practices that no longer serve the needs of students today.

To avoid mode locking, we must look to a different form of leadership. We must view leadership in the context of relationships. Margaret Wheatley, in *Leadership and the New Science* (1992), writes,

Leaders are being encouraged to include stakeholders, to evoke followership, to empower others. . . . Leadership is *always* dependent on the context but the context is established by the *relationships* we value. We cannot hope to influence any situation without respect for the complex network of people who contribute to our organizations. (p. 144)

Collaborative leadership offers the kind of leadership Margaret Wheatley has described as always dependent on the context established by the relationships of the members of the organization. It is in this context that the skills of the Five Essentials transpose traditional leadership forms into a relational form of collaborative leadership. Collaborative leadership makes it possible to subject information to dynamic and interactive discussions of the stakeholders of an organization.

As Wheatley points out, "The function of information is revealed in the word itself: in-formation" (1992, p. 104). The state of this new organizational form, sympathetic to the Five Essentials, is itself "in-formation." Constantly exhibiting robustness, as Gleick describes, this form of organization can withstand small jolts generated by changing needs and growing diversity. This new form of school organization mixes a view of information, defined by constant change as it regenerates itself, with a view of relationships that reflects underlying value of the organizational stakeholders. What we need is an opening up to this new and emerging ebb and flow of organizational dynamics, founded upon valuing the contributions of the stakeholders and turning information into intelligence that is flexible yet bounded by parameters entrusted to the stakeholders to determine.

Calling upon chaos theory provides (1) some insights for new organizational forms and (2) a new meaning for leadership. Wheatley (1992) describes a phenomenon from the new science known as a strange attractor:

A strange attractor is a basin of attraction, an area displayed in computer-generated phase space that the system is magnetically driven into, pulling the system into a visible shape. . . . In a chaotic system, scientists now can observe movements that, though random and unpredictable, never exceed finite boundaries. (p. 122)

For organizational transformations, chaos theory teaches us that what appears as chaos and lack of control has implicitly an underlying order. Our traditional reactions to what appears as chaos in an organization in transformation are to resist it and restore that which went before. Resistance to change is strongly rooted in a need to restore order. But it is this very natural tendency we must resist, not the apparent chaos itself. We must know and trust that there are order and boundaries to what appears as chaotic, and the emergence of a transformed collaborative organization is the reward for this tolerance of ambiguity.

What does this transformed organization look like? The smallest part of the organization is intimately related to the whole. Briggs and Peat, in their book, *Turbulent Mirror: An Illustrated Guide to Chaos Theory and the Science of Wholeness,* suggest that, "The whole shape of things depends on the minutest part. The part *is* the whole in this respect, for through the action of any part, the whole in the form of chaos or transformative change may manifest" (1989, pp. 74–75). As it is with the universe, so it is with organizational transformation. Transforming an organization with the integration of the Five Essentials brings with it the notion that the smallest part reflects the nature of the whole.

Margaret Wheatley (1992) discusses how fractals reflect the comparison of the part to the whole. She describes them in this manner:

> The most beautiful images of iteration are found in the artistry of fractals, computer generated models drawn by the iteration of a few equations. . . . Everywhere in this minutely detailed fractal landscape, there is self similarity . . . There is pattern within pattern within pattern. (pp. 127–128)

Fractals have implications for organizational transformation. There is a reflection of wholeness within a high performing organization. You can feel it from the smallest division to the overall clearly defined purpose that emanates from both its leadership and individual stakeholders.

Wheatley (1992) describes it this way:

> I believe that fractals also have direct application for the leadership of organizations. The very best organizations have a fractal quality to them. An observer of such an organization can tell what the organization's values and ways of doing business are by watching anyone. (p. 132)

There is a natural trust between the stakeholders within these organizations. And it is the Five Essentials that can best generate this trust everywhere within the organization. Stakeholders trained in the Five Essentials develop collaborative relationships that ultimately reflect a quality of behavior to be found everywhere in the organization. There develops a fractal nature of similar behaviors.

THE FIVE ESSENTIALS
AND SCHOOL CULTURE

Although they are anchored in competence and skills, the Five Essentials go beyond these abilities. Their implementation, along with the accompanying competence and skills, helps transform an organization into a proactive one. This proactive profile provides the seed beds for the flourishing of creativity among the organizational stakeholders. Committed individuals embrace the natural inclination to be creative and productive, which resides in all of us.

In order to help transform a school in this way, building principals need to provide the leadership necessary for the development of a "transformation culture" within their school. Much has been written concerning managing versus leading. Whereas the successful operation of a school calls for a careful balance of both managing and leading, it is the leadership ability of the principal that is crucial to the creation of the organizational culture necessary for school transformation. In his book *Mind of a Manager, Soul of a Leader*, Craig Hickman points out,

> While both managers and leaders may recognize the value of both strategy and culture in an organization, managers tend to think of the strategy-culture mix from the strategic perspective, while leaders tend to see the mix from the cultural side. This happens because strategic lends itself to analysis, the systematic generation of alternatives, and calculated decision making. Culture, on the other hand, involves inspiration, value sharing, and deep sensitivity to capabilities. By nature, the manager's mind favors clear-cut courses of action based on the implementation of a specific, detailed plan to resolve an issue. The leader's soul, on the other hand, naturally favors creating a cultural climate and attitude conducive to resolving an issue through an appropriate course of action. (1990, p. 55)

In order to create a transformational school culture, the building principal must develop a finely tuned ability to recognize capabilities in each of the stakeholders, and most important, in the teachers. It is the principal's responsibility to inspire stakeholders to reach and accomplish well beyond that which they would accomplish in the principal's absence.

In order to effectively share values and inspire those around him or her, a building principal must unlearn many traditional organizational practices, such as delegating. Warren Bennis and Robert Townsend, in their book *Reinventing Leadership: Strategies to Empower the Organization* (1995), point out the need to revisit traditional practices:

> I want to reframe the issue of delegation. The word sounds strangely quaint and rustic to me. *Delegate* sounds like I'm going to give a job to somebody else, who's working for me, to do. When you think about management today you think about a team of people. You think about a boss or leader and a group. Delegating gets to be more complicated.

They way I used to run things, and I think the way very effective leaders do, too, is the following. List a set of functions that the organization or group needs to get done. What are the group's primary tasks? List also what people feel they want to do. And third, list what they're competent doing. Now, if you can get the right mixture of what needs to be done, what people want to do, and what they're competent to do, I think you'll have a high performing, fully empowered team. That reframes the whole issue of delegation, because it's basically a team effort and not just the boss handing off the work, like a quarterback handing off the ball to a running back. That kind of delegation is not simple. But I do think we're going to have to enlarge the concept of delegation to a team effort that the leader can encourage. (pp. 81–82)

The challenge of transforming a school, utilizing the Five Essentials, is to build new competencies within the stakeholders. This responsibility falls mainly to the building principal. The building principal must be capable of recognizing traditional barriers to the creation of new and better accommodations for learner needs and eliminate them wherever they are found. In order to create the culture necessary to transform a school into one with a profile of high performance, the school building principal must

- Facilitate the development of the five essential skills within the stakeholders.
- Provide the opportunity to share values.
- Encourage the school stakeholders to "reach" and take risks.
- Use techniques such as conjoining conversation (see Chapter 1) to actively and meaningfully engage the school stakeholders.
- Create a transformation team and communicate an appreciation of individual stakeholder contributions of ideas.
- Eliminate administrative arrangements from the past that are not flexible enough to accommodate innovations and creative approaches on the part of school stakeholders.

When school principals make a commitment to transformational leadership and practices, an environment is created in which stakeholders are willing to go beyond traditional expectations to accomplish the vision of the school.

Henry P. Sims, Jr. and Charles C. Manz, in their book entitled *Company of Heroes*, point out, "Inspirational persuasion is a closely related behavior to exhortation. The leader combines words that create images, energy, and emotion to persuade followers to adhere to the values and pursue (the vision) the leader has communicated" (1996, p. 48). Without question, the creation of a school culture capable of transforming the organization into one with a high performance profile is dependent upon (1) the ability of the principal to provide transformational leadership and (2) the presence of conversation among the stakeholders that is rich with creative ideas and the combined wisdom of all. Sims and Manz go on to say, "The idea is to use the power of words to move others to commit, of their own will, to what the leader wants. . . . Once persuasion succeeds, followers are programmed from within" (p. 48).

Some of the natural flow and rhythms of the organizational workplace contribute to the accomplishment of the mission and some do not. The skills of the Five Essentials help differentiate between these rhythms. The spirit of the Five Essentials is a reflection of the human spirit. With the Five Essentials integrated firmly into an organization, a culture is created based upon commonly understood and commonly accepted expectations and values that in turn shape and form organizational behavior.

Terrence E. Deal and Kent D. Peterson, in their book *Shaping School Culture: The Heart of Leadership* (1998), put it this way:

> This invisible, taken-for-granted flow of beliefs and assumptions gives meaning to what people say and do. It shapes how they interpret hundreds of daily transactions. This deeper structure of life in organizations is reflected and transmitted through symbolic language and expressive action. Culture consists of the stable underlying social meanings that shape beliefs and behavior over time. (p. 3)

Transforming a school into an organizational form that incorporates the Five Essentials flushes traditional and tacit assumptions regarding unwritten rules, policies, and unspoken expectations. In the transformed organization, these tacit and unspoken factors are thoroughly discussed, and decisions regarding justifying or abandoning each of them produce an organizational profile that is far more effective at accomplishing the organizational mission.

We can characterize the contributions the Five Essentials make to an organizational culture as follows:

• From Planning Strategically: A strong sense of predictability is infused within the culture of the organization. At any point in time, each stakeholder knows where the organization is and where it is going. More important, they know why.

• From Benchmarking for Excellence: The stakeholders develop a strong sense of individual and organizational expertise. Stakeholders come to understand high performance and what it takes to get there. Their sense of professional pride becomes grounded in measurable positive results.

• From Collaborative Leadership: Stakeholders develop a strong sense of collegiality and a personal investment in the combined wisdom of collaborative decision making. They come to understand that what they think, believe, and know can and will make an impact on final decisions affecting them and their organization.

• From Governance by Standards: Stakeholders develop a positive and productive level of comfort born of a sense of order. Rules and policies are mutually developed and commonly accepted. Throughout the organization, there is a sense of fair and even-handed treatment when governed by standards representing commonly defined excellence in their industry.

• From Public Engagement: Stakeholders develop a sense of shared purpose and mutual support among and between the school and community. A positive spirit develops between schools and their public. The productive culture of an organization is dependent upon the effective leadership of that organization. The literature in this area is replete with the importance of the leader to communicate, on an ongoing basis, organizational values and guiding visions. These organizational values and guiding visions, in turn, need to reflect the input of the organizational members. This is a process that is never complete in a learning organization.

THE FIVE ESSENTIALS AND LEARNING ORGANIZATIONS

Peter Senge et al., in *The Fifth Discipline Field Book* (1994), discuss learning organizations in terms of great teams. They make the point that great teams never start out that way but merely as a group of individuals. Senge et al. put it like this:

> Great teams are learning organizations—groups of people who, over time, enhance their capacity to create what they truly desire to create. . . . Team members develop new skills and capabilities which alter what they can do and understand. . . .
>
> This deep learning cycle constitutes the essence of a learning organization—the development not just of new capacities, but of fundamental shifts of mind, individually and collectively. The five basic learning disciplines are the means by which this deep learning cycle is activated. (p. 18)

The five basic learning disciplines to which Senge et al. refer are Systems Thinking, Personal Mastery, Mental Models, Shared Vision, and Team Learning. They offer the following descriptions of these five disciplines:

> By its nature, Systems Thinking points out interdependencies and the need for collaboration. Thus, as the team continues its work, it

may become necessary to bring in new members—particularly people who were once seen as enemies, but are now obviously players on the same side of the game. (1994, p. 92)

Collaborative leadership and the impact of the knowledge of personality types facilitate the development of functional interdependencies described by Senge et al. The effectiveness of the relationships between individuals begins with self-knowledge. Senge et al. describe their notion of Personal Mastery as follows:

Developing a personal vision means tapping into a deep well of hope and aspiration, ...
　　To provide conditions in which individuals can develop their capacity to create what they care about, organizations must invest time, energy, and money. . . . Personal mastery implies a willingness to invest what is necessary to create an environment that helps employees become high-quality contributors. (1994, p. 199)

It is the responsibility of leadership to help create a work environment in which it is possible for organizational members to accomplish their personal goals while in the process of accomplishing the organizational mission. Senge's explanation of personal mastery and the requirements of the organization that would support it are congruent with the requirements of collaborative leadership and meaningful engagement of the organizational stakeholders. Shared visions for an organization begin with personal visions of its members. Senge et al. describe Shared Visions as follows:

Thus, at the heart of the shared vision is the task of designing and evolving ongoing processes in which people. . . can speak from the heart about what really matters to them and be heard by senior management and each other. (1994, p. 299)

The relationships within an organization begin with conversation between its members—all members. In order for people at every level of the organization to develop the necessary trust required to speak from the heart, they must share positive experiences as this process begins. Training in collaborative leadership and stakeholder engagement provides the necessary skills for the stakeholders to trust enough and feel comfortable enough to arrive at a truly shared vision of the organization. The pathway to this shared vision is the combination of individual visions, collaboratively developed. Through the discussions required to reach a shared vision, mental models are revealed. Senge et al. describe Mental Models as follows:

Mental models are the images, assumptions, and stories which we carry in our minds of ourselves, other people, institutions, and every aspect of the world. . . . [M]ental models determine what we see.

But because mental models are usually *tacit* . . . they are often untested and unexamined. . . . The core task of this discipline is bringing mental models to the surface . . . to help us . . . find ways to re-form . . . new mental models that serve us better in the world. (1994, pp. 235–236)

Mental models, like personality types, reflect how we as individuals see things differently. However, if we are to come to a common vision of an organization as a whole, we must arrive at a shared meaning incrementally, conversation by conversation, decision by decision. Whether the subject involves planning, benchmarking, governing, or any other subject, we begin by sharing perceptions, knowing they are influenced by mental models as Senge et al. have suggested. We must learn to work through the ambiguity created by this enterprise in order to reach the degree of comfort necessary to open up to influencing and, in turn, being influenced by one another.

Nothing succeeds like success. Collaborative leadership skills provide the potential for organizational members to break free of outdated and biased mental models. Experiencing the success of benchmarking for high performance or referencing the objectivity of standards-based decision making serve as just two examples of the myriad of ways we can learn to come together successfully by inventing new mental models that are more consistent with what the organization is becoming than with what it has been.

Senge et al. describe Team Learning as deeply rooted in a focus on the worthiness of individual members of the organization:

This discipline inspires more fundamental changes, with enduring application that will ripple out through the organization. . . . The process of learning how to learn collectively is unfamiliar. . . . It starts with self-mastery and self-knowledge, but involves looking outward to develop knowledge of, and alignment with, others on your team. (1994, pp. 355–356).

The quality of relationships among members is of paramount importance to team learning within a learning organization.

SUMMARY

Chaos theory offers clues to a simpler way to lead organizations. What we know about strange attractors and fractals from the "new science" has implications for school organizational forms and leadership. "Mode locking" from natural science may explain why school organizations have not readily adapted to change.

Changing school cultures and changing school leadership go hand in hand. You cannot improve one without improving the other. The productive culture of an organization is dependent upon the effective leadership of that organization. In turn, the effective leadership of the organization is dependent on the effective implementation of the skills of the Five Essentials.

One of the best ways to meet the challenge of developing a productive school culture is to establish collaborative decision making within that culture. Collaborative decision making begins with conversation. Stakeholders skilled in the Five Essentials are able to quickly turn their conversations into collaborative discussions. How we combine discipline with these discussions to produce collaborative dialogue is the subject of the next chapter.

10

Conclusion

*When followership and leadership are joined, the traditional
hierarchy of the school is upset.*

—Thomas J. Sergiovanni (1992)

THE LEADERSHIP TRAP

I was never comfortable with the traditional trappings of "leadership."
People will define your leadership persona if you allow it. A leader must
quickly learn the difference between the mission of the school district and
the political agendas of those who seek narrow and special interest favors
from the power of the position. One way to easily make the distinction is
to seek out those who relate to you as the person that you *are* as opposed
to the *position* that you hold.

Among other characteristics of leadership, leaders should view themselves as "enablers." To encourage collaboration in a discussion, leaders
must model collaborative skills. To get the most meaningful engagement
of the stakeholders, leaders must engage. To facilitate within the stakeholders the desire and skills to embrace benchmarking for excellence, governing by standards, and strategic planning, the leader must model
benchmarking, administering by standards, and planning strategically.

If you allow it, others will mold your leadership into a traditional
mode, focusing on power instead of empowerment, special interest
instead of student interest, talking instead of listening, directing instead of

facilitating, and individual thought instead of collective wisdom. Indeed, leadership today requires a healthy dose of "professional ego-strength" if one is to stay the course toward transformation.

THE DISCIPLINE OF DIALOGUE

When confronted with difficult problems and challenges, without a collaborative mindset, it becomes easy, almost natural, to fall into the "we, they" mentality. "They simply won't understand" or "They are not personally invested" become easy judgments to exonerate us from blame or failure. In an almost natural manner, we stick blame fast and firm to others (they). Or is it so natural? We must learn to strike a balance between the "discipline of dialogue," defined below, and the responsibility to understand others.

Joseph Jaworski, in his book *Synchronicity: The Inner Path of Leadership*, points out that, "In the heat of the creative process, we end up having so much to do that we lose the necessary orientation to stay in the flow. Unless we have the individual and collective discipline to continually stay anchored, we will lose the flow" (1996, p. 129). He goes on to say, "That's why the discipline of dialogue seems to be so important for everyone in such an enterprise. Taking the time to come together on a regular basis in true dialogue gives everyone a chance to maintain a reflective space at the heart of the activity—a space where all people can continue to be re-nurtured together by what is wanting to happen, to unfold" (1996, pp. 129–130).

There is a natural flow and rhythm to collaborative dialogue. It becomes almost synchronous to those skilled in the process. Solutions to problems evolve through such dialogue. The productivity of collaborative dialogue is facilitated by knowledge of the Five Essentials. With knowledge of the Five Essentials, participants can more effectively arrive at a common meaning and understanding.

HAVE YOU TOLD THEM THAT?

The skills of the Five Essentials clearly overlap. The mental attitude that facilitates acquiring these skills might be described as "Grandma's common sense." Cooperation, equal treatment, fairness, open-mindedness, do unto others as you would have them do unto you, describe a few of the qualities that Grandma might exhibit. Being comfortable with your communication is important to essential skills development. When someone complains of the behavior of another staff member, an appropriate response would be, "Have you told this person what you just told me?" Their most likely answer is that they could never do that, that it would be too embarrassing and seemingly cruel. But it does not have to be that way—It is not *what* you tell the person, but *how*, that determines whether the criticism you bring them is supportive. Your message should be delivered in a broad context of the positive as well as the negative behavior you were observing. As we communicate, it is our responsibility to initiate an exchange of a personal investment in the other party. We must eliminate the threat of intimidation in our message. Good friends certainly learn how to do this, and indeed this skill is at the heart of "good friendship." So it should be with collaborative colleagues.

Behavior is based upon perception. If your perception of the "truth" is different from their perception, you must attempt to understand what they see. The perception and behavior will then take on new meaning. Understanding this "hidden meaning" represents the first step in changing perception, which in turn is the trigger to changing behavior.

Recall the first time you heard your voice on a tape recorder, or saw yourself on a videotape. Most people are shocked with the unanticipated impact these experiences bring. Your perception of your own behavior is often different from how others perceive you. The key to effectively putting the Five Essentials to work for you and your organization is to make certain that your behavior and the meaning of your words are perceived as you intended them. You must listen deeply and empathically to those around you to make sure that your intentions are congruent with others' perceptions of what you say and do.

CHANGING TIMES, CHANGING CHALLENGES

In order to meet the challenges of a clearly changing society, Terrence Deal and Kent Peterson, in *Shaping School Culture: The Heart Of Leadership* (1999), caution the leadership of the future. They present their notion of future opportunities and challenges in the following way:

> *Opportunity of purpose.* Central to successful schools is a powerful sense of purpose that is focused on students and on learning. Developing and articulating a deep sense of purpose is the foundation of a strong culture.

> *Opportunity of place.* Schools are complex, demanding institutions. School leaders must make these special places where students, staff, parents, and community members feel welcome, safe, and appreciated. . . .

> *Opportunity of people.* People are the central resource in any organization. When leaders invest in a culture that nurtures and challenges

staff, students, and community, it pays off in learning outcomes. Putting time into building a culture that motivates and inspires people is the venture capital of schools.

Opportunity of competence. Human beings crave competence. Everyone wants to do well. The challenge and opportunity for school leaders is to nourish the competence of the staff and students in their work, their thinking, and their daily actions. Through competence comes achievement.

Opportunity of commitment. School leaders will need to build or, in some cases, resurrect commitment to schools and to education. The past decade has disheartened some about the possibilities of education and the potential of schools. School leaders from every corner of the school need to relentlessly build commitment.

Opportunity of celebration. School leaders need to find exciting ways to celebrate accomplishments of the culture. Schools are living, breathing organisms. In order to thrive, people need to come together in community to celebrate accomplishment, hard work, and dedication. (pp. 139–140)

School leaders of tomorrow must understand that the investment of time and energy in the human resources of a school district is the best investment for organizational development. The road to organizational excellence is paved with the development of conceptual understanding and deeply felt beliefs in the meaning of the organization. The culture of the organization is a reflection of the shared meanings and common understandings of the stakeholders. The quality of the culture will be no better than the combined quality of the relationships of the organizational members.

CAPTAIN EDUCATION

Albert Einstein is often quoted as stating, "No problem can be solved from the same consciousness that created it." We must learn new rhythms and orchestrations of the symphony of change to grow our school organizations into what they can be. Our ability to synthesize new designs and initiatives to transform our schools is dependent on this. We must add to our store of building blocks by not only thinking differently but by acting differently as well. We can replace rancor with excitement, sarcasm with praise, and the isolation of "silo thinking" with the blending of combined wisdom.

Approaching the changes required on the part of the stakeholders to execute the transformation of an organization requires the development of a new mentality relative to attitudes and beliefs. In their book entitled *Fusion Leadership,* Richard Daft and Robert Lengel (1998) describe "leader mindfulness" as "being willing to stand apart, to say what you believe, to have opinions, to determine your course by your inner rudder rather than by your external rudder. Managers often steer their course by determining what is acceptable to bosses and the peer culture. They use a technique like radar, learning what other people think before deciding their own path. Mindful leaders determine their path by what they believe from within. They trust the subtle inner voice of creativity and independent thought" (p. 76).

There resides a "Captain Education" in every educator. Constraints from the past and our own experience prevent us from unleashing the power of our own unique Captain Education. Only by developing a collective conscience of improved learning opportunities for students can we begin to transform our school districts. The Five Essentials hold the key to this transformation. The work is not easy, but the results are most gratifying.

WHAT NOW?

The time has come to refocus governance and leadership in American elementary and secondary schools, and staff development programs represent the starting point for this transformation. In order to develop the skills of the Five Essentials, public schools need to reallocate resources from areas of spending and utilization not contributing to the accomplishment of the school mission to areas, such as training in the Five Essentials, that do. In this way, we can initiate and sustain the transformation of schools.

But there is more. The transformation of schools begins with a transformation of individuals and relationships. We can begin by recognizing that what we have recently discovered about high-performing organizations is that their beginnings are rooted in conversation, in dialogue between individuals. The whole group is the sum of individuals dedicated to a common meaning and understanding of the "fractal" nature and purpose of the organization.

The leaders of schools today must recognize that developing high-performing students comes down to developing high-performing stakeholders (parents, teachers, and administrators). It is through knowing and practicing collaborative leadership skills that first steps by school leaders are taken.

But there is still more. Mindsets, what Peter Senge calls "mental models," must change from the firmly bounded notion of leadership rooted in the past to the flexible, open, and receptive model of collaborative leadership for tomorrow. Parents can collaborate, teachers can lead, and administrators can follow. In the ebb and flow—the rhythms—of creative dialogue, there is the need to listen to our inner voice, the nature of which is to form collective mindsets and collaborative wisdom. This is the meaning of working together in high-performing organizations.

Transforming or restructuring schools follows individual transformations. It is important to break down "silos of independent thought" and administrative arrangements from the past that no longer serve the needs for which they were intended. However, it is more important to create a school culture that facilitates individual and personal commitment to realize the creative potential residing in all of us.

In each of the areas of the Five Essentials, there must be a reflection of the personal investment of the stakeholders in maximizing their performance. This happens through honest and sincere opportunities to both be heard and to listen. The whole is defined by the parts. The bridge from individual performance excellence to high organizational performance is greatly strengthened by the development of the Five Essential Skills. The total contribution of the development of these skills is far greater than the sum of their individual contributions. What now needs to happen is school leaders must initiate the dedication of both their spirit and organizational resources to this enterprise.

SUMMARY

The promise of improved student learning opportunities is dependent upon the effective transformation of school organizations. Transforming organizations mixes many ingredients, none more important than people. Understanding relationships requires deep listening skills, none more important than person-to-person. Finally, designing school transformations enjoin a confluence of people, conceptual understandings, and commitment to a commonly derived meaning of the organization. The Five Essentials provide the skills necessary to work our way through the challenge of organizational transformation.

Epilogue
A Sense of Urgency

In times of crisis, organizational members can often "pull together," ignore everyday differences, and demonstrate amazing ability to meet the crisis and restore normalcy. Why is this? Peter Senge refers to "creative tension" (1994, p. 195) as the tension that is created when we both hold a personal vision and discover a difference between it and our view of the current reality before us. Senge asserts that the only way to ease this tension is to take initiative to move the current reality closer to our personal vision. Certainly, many would agree that a sense of urgency often acts as a motivator and incentive to change reality.

Within learning organizations, it is important for cross-functional teams of organizational stakeholders to not only arrive at a shared vision of the organization, but also to come to share a similar sense of urgency related to moving the current organizational reality closer to that shared vision. Developing and practicing the skills of the Five Essentials, and applying them to the process of collaboratively sharing and discussing personal visions, represents the first step in moving organizational realities closer to a collective vision of the organization. As collaborative teams of stakeholders set about the process of understanding deeply rooted personal beliefs and attitudes, the guiding visions and organizational beliefs of the organization emerge. The strength of these organizational beliefs and values is found in the personal commitment generated within the organizational members by the process used to discover them. Stakeholders thus become engaged and committed.

UNDERLYING SIMPLICITY

There is an underlying simplicity inherent in the development of a high-performing learning organization. This simplicity can be found in the collaborative process. We must learn to deal in the currency of conceptual understanding. Controlling rules and regulations that typify highly structured organizations stymie the flexibility and responsiveness needed today in order to shape learning organizations. This requires a different kind of leadership—a collaborative leadership.

Chaos theory teaches us that what appears chaotic in nature in reality reflects a simple underlying structure and order. We should view "strange attractors," movements in a system that appear to be chaotic but never go beyond predictable limits, as empowering, not chaotic. It is empowering for school organizations to free stakeholders to experiment with new organizational forms as well as new ways of doing business. The skills of the Five Essentials help provide the keys to unlocking the infinite potential residing within school organizational stakeholders across our nation. School leaders must learn to trust that a shared organizational meaning among the stakeholders will serve as the "basin of attraction" to keep what may appear to be chaotic organizational development efforts within acceptable boundaries. For example, the focus of the training of a school district may shift from short-term, content-oriented workshops to longer-term, leadership-skills development academies. The "payoff" may not be observable in the short term and may even appear chaotic at times. However, the long-term benefits of applying the collaborative leadership skills of the Five Essentials to the problems and challenges of the school district shape its positive transformation. Because of their shared meaning of the organization, as stakeholders experiment and innovate with new forms of improving student learning potential, their initiatives will always respect these boundaries, so defined. Once established, a learning organization will reveal its fractal nature by demonstrating the unique behavior patterns and organizational processes that are similar at every level of the organization. The similarity of behavior of all of the stakeholders will reflect a quality and orientation unique to the meaning and purpose of the organization.

LEADING FOR CHANGE

There is no question that school leadership of this century will be called upon to develop new skills and attitudes that facilitate the development of collaborative learning organizations. What follows is a list of the skills and attitudes necessary to meet this challenge:

1. Recognize that human resource development is the cornerstone of the implementation of programs and services necessary to increase learning opportunities and student achievement. The Five Essentials form the basis of improving the skills of the stakeholders to develop new organizational forms. The purpose of these new . organizational forms is to tap more effectively into the human potential of the organizational stakeholder.

2. Develop a tolerance for ambiguity necessary to break with traditional organizational forms in order to create new and improved organizational systems. The most difficult challenges do not have easily derived solutions. The process of searching for new organizational forms will naturally cause some doubt and uncertainty along the way. It is the collaborative efforts of the stakeholders that produce more flexible mindsets which in turn help eliminate some of this doubt. In addition, it is the combined wisdom of the stakeholders that offers the most potentially effective initiatives for improvement.

3. Teach and allow others to lead. Encourage the stakeholders to be innovative and collaborative, recognizing that leadership and followership are intimately related and both are based upon quality relationships between the organizational stakeholders.

4. Understand differences between personality types within the organizational members. Use these differences as a source of strength for transforming the organization.

5. Employ public engagement principles to authentically incorporate the best thinking of all stakeholders.

I have attempted to describe the most important and difficult educational issues confronting public schools today. The Five Essentials address these issues. Each requires the development of skills necessary to transform schools.

Human resource development is the conduit through which we deliver these essential skills to schools. Training, such as that discussed under "Local Leadership Academy" in Chapter 4, in which the skills of the Five Essentials are taught in an ongoing manner, should become a major focus of the human resource department. In addition, training in the Five Essentials should involve all the stakeholders of public schools and, most important, it should involve school board members, parents, teachers, and administrators. Training in these skills constitutes training in leadership itself. The root word of education is the Latin term *educare*—to lead. Leadership and education are intimately related. To educate is to lead, and it should happen at all levels of school organizations. If the transformation of our schools is to be a success, leadership training is essential.

References

Attenborough, R. (Producer/Director). (1982). *Gandhi* [Motion Picture]. Burbank, CA: Columbia Pictures.

Bennis, W., & Townsend, R. (1995). *Reinventing leadership: Strategies to empower the organization.* New York: William Morrow.

Blazey, M. L. (1999). *Insights to performance excellence, 1999: An inside look at the 1999 Baldrige Award Criteria.* Milwaukee, WI: ASQ Quality Press.

Briggs, J., & Peat, F. D. (1989). *Turbulent mirror: An illustrated guide to chaos theory and the science of wholeness.* New York: Harper and Row.

Bryson, J. M. (1995). *Strategic planning for public and nonprofit organizations.* San Francisco: Jossey-Bass.

Capra, F. (1983). *The turning point: Science, society, and the rising culture.* New York: Bantam.

Covey, S. R. (1990a). *Principle-centered leadership.* New York: Simon & Schuster.

Covey, S. R. (1990b). *The seven habits of highly effective people.* New York: Simon & Schuster.

Daft, R. L., & Lengel, R. H. (1998). *Fusion leadership.* San Francisco: Barrett-Koehler.

Deal, T. E., & Peterson, Kent D. (1998). *Shaping school culture: The heart of leadership.* San Francisco: Jossey-Bass.

Feddema, H. J. (1996). *Internal coordinator's guide: A practical guide for developing and implementing a strategic plan from inside your school district.* Montgomery, AL: The Cambridge Group.

Florida Sterling Council. (2000). *The 2000 Sterling Criteria for Organizational Performance Excellence.* Tallahassee, FL: Author.

Frankl, V. (1959). *Man's search for meaning.* Boston: Beacon.

George, S. (1992). *The Baldrige Quality System.* New York: John Wiley.

Gleick, J. (1987). *Chaos: Making a new science.* New York: Penguin.

Goleman, D., Boyatzis, R., & McKee, A. (2002). *Primal leadership: Realizing the power of emotional intelligence.* Boston: Harvard Business School Press.

Handy, C. (1996). *Beyond certainty.* Boston: Harvard Business School Press.

Handy, C. (1997). *The hungry spirit.* London: Hutchinson.

Harrington, H. J., & Harrington, J. S. (1996). *High performance benchmarking.* New York: McGraw-Hill.

Harwood, R. C., Perry, M. J., & Schmitt, W. G. (1993). *Meaningful chaos: How people form relationships with public concerns.* Dayton, Ohio: Kettering Foundation.

Hickman, C. R. (1990). *Mind of a manager, soul of a leader.* New York: John Wiley.

Jaworski, J. (1996). *Synchronicity, The inner path of leadership.* San Francisco: Berrett-Koehler.

Johnson, J., & Immerwahr, J. (1994). *First things first: What Americans expect from the public schools.* New York: Public Agenda.

Kahaner, L. (1996). *Competitive intelligence: How to gather, analyze, and use information to move your business to the top.* New York: Simon & Schuster.

Kline, P., & Saunders, B. (1993). *Ten steps to a learning organization.* Arlington, VA: Great Ocean.

Kroeger, O., & Thuesen, J. M. (1992). *Type talk at work.* New York: Dell.

Lawler, E. L. (1991). *High involvement management.* San Francisco: Jossey-Bass.

Maxwell, J. C. (1999). *The 21 indispensable qualities of a leader.* Nashville, TN: Thomas Nelson.

McGregor, D. (1960). *The human side of enterprise.* New York: McGraw-Hill.

Murphy, E. C. (1996). *Leadership I.Q.* New York: John Wiley.

Myers, I. B., McCaulley, M. H., Quenk, N. L., & Hammer, A. L. (1998). *MBTI manual: A guide to the development and use of the Myers-Briggs Type Indicator.* Palo Alto, CA: Consulting Psychologists Press.

Schorr, L. B. (1997). *Common purpose.* New York: Doubleday.

Schlechty, P. C. (1997) *Inventing better schools: An action plan for education reform.* San Francisco: Jossey-Bass.

Schrage, M. (1995). *No more teams: Mastering the dynamics of creative collaboration.* New York: Doubleday.

Senge, P. M. (1990). *The fifth discipline: The art and practice of the learning organization.* New York: Doubleday.

Senge, P. M., Kleiner, A., Roberts, C., Ross, R., Roth, G., & Smith, B. (1999). *The dance of change.* New York: Doubleday.

Senge, P. M., Roberts, C., Ross, R. B., Smith, B. J., & Kleiner, A. (1994). *The fifth discipline fieldbook.* New York: Doubleday.

Sergiovanni, T. J. (1992). *Moral leadership: Getting to the heart of school improvement.* San Francisco: Jossey-Bass.

Sims, H. P., Jr., & Manz, C. C. (1996). *Company of heroes: Unleashing the power of self-leadership.* New York: John Wiley.

Smith, G. P. (1997). *The new leader: Bringing creativity and innovation to the workplace.* Boca Raton, FL: St. Lucie Press.

Terry, R. W. (1993). *Authentic leadership: Courage in action.* San Francisco: Jossey-Bass.

Wheatley, M. J. (1992). *Leadership and the new science.* San Francisco: Berrett-Koehler.

Index

**CORWIN
PRESS**

The Corwin Press logo—a raven striding across an open book—represents the happy union of courage and learning. We are a professional-level publisher of books and journals for K-12 educators, and we are committed to creating and providing resources that embody these qualities. Corwin's motto is "Success for All Learners."